CHRISTMAS CRAFT
SOURCE BOOK

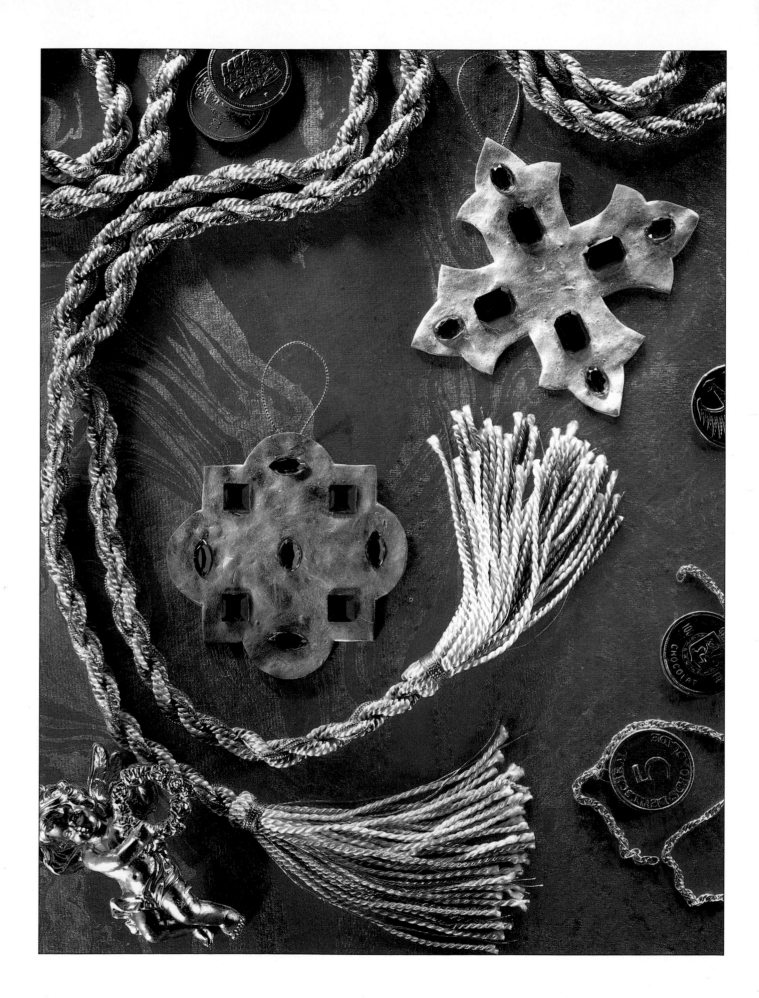

CHRISTMAS CRAFT
SOURCE BOOK

GAIL LAWTHER

Trafalgar Square Publishing

First published in the United States of America in 1995 by
Trafalgar Square Publishing, North Pomfret, Vermont 05053

First published in Great Britain in 1994 by
Anaya Publishers Ltd, London

Printed and bound in China

Editor: Patsy North
Designer: Sheila Volpe
Special photography: Lucinda Symons
Stylist: Katherine Yeates
Artwork: Michael Volpe, Kate Simunek

ISBN 1-57076-019-5
Library of Congress Catalog Card Number: 94-61663

Typeset by Servis Filmsetting Ltd, Manchester, UK
Colour reproduction by J. Film Process Pre Ltd, Singapore
Produced by Mandarin Offset

CONTENTS

INTRODUCTION

Christmas: a time to celebrate. For virtually everyone, the Christmas holiday is a time for decorations, good food, parties, and whatever customs or activities mean the most to them, whether it is going to a seasonal play or ballet, decorating the cake or attending Midnight Mass. And most of us feel the urge to decorate our homes to make them look special for the Christmas season. Traditional decorations always have a strong appeal, but there are times when some of the favourite baubles break or you realize that the crib scene you have been using for years is really past its best. Or perhaps you just want to make something new to give your house a different look for Christmas.

In this book you will find many ideas for Christmas decorations of every kind, as well as hundreds of new motifs for making your own designs. Each chapter has a section of trace-off line drawings with suggestions for ways of using the motifs, which can be enlarged or reduced on a photocopier for even more versatility. Throughout the book I have chosen beautiful Christmas items to illustrate some of the motifs and crafts that I talk about. These range from wonderful textured machine embroideries and elaborate papercrafts to simple stencilled designs, wreaths, cards and tree decorations that you can easily make yourself in an hour or two. At the end of the book, in *Materials and Techniques*, I explain how to tackle papercrafts, modelling and other crafts successfully. As well as the ideas that you will find here, tear out pages from magazines that feature Christmas designs, and keep the best of your cards and cuttings of interesting wrapping papers. If you slip them into a plastic wallet and keep them with this book, you will have all your resources together for reference when Christmas comes round once again.

Involving children in the preparations for Christmas is half the fun, and they will enjoy using many of the ideas here. You may find it very useful to sit them down at a table with craft materials and some photostats from the book, while you get on with some of the more complicated preparations – or sneak away to buy or wrap their presents! Make sure that all the equipment they use is safe and suitable for their age-group, then you won't have to worry about letting them come up with their own creations.

As a background to each chapter I talk about many of the traditions associated with certain yuletide symbols or customs, and explain why each of them has come to be linked with Christmas – why, for instance, do we sing carols? And why do we think of candles as being particularly appropriate for Christmas? Why don't churches include mistletoe among their Christmas greenery? And, talking of mistletoe, how many kisses can you have under the mistletoe sprig?

The character of Christmas has evolved over the centuries. The very date itself is no more likely to be the exact day when Jesus was born than virtually any other day of the year; it was chosen from several other contenders, partly because it coincided with the midwinter festivals that were

already celebrated. Somehow it wouldn't have seemed the same celebrating Christmas on January 2nd, April 18th or 19th, or May 20th – all put forward as suggestions in earlier centuries. During the time of Cromwell in England, Christmas celebrations were banned, right down to the eating of mince pies, or going to church if December 25th didn't fall on a Sunday. Even if most of us agree that Christmas has become too commercialized, I don't think that any of us would want to return to those puritanical days!

The most important thing about Christmas is to enjoy it. It is all too easy to find yourself becoming a slave to the celebrations, rather than giving yourself time to appreciate them. If the family doesn't want a big Christmas dinner, don't cook one; if you'd rather decorate your house with shiny silver cardboard angels than sophisticated evergreen wreaths, then do. Don't let your Christmas decorations and arrangements become a tyranny; relax, enjoy yourself, try out a few new things and, above all, have a lot of fun.

ABOVE *Christmas items are very rewarding to make and add a unique touch to your decorations.*

Chapter 1

THE CHRISTMAS TREE

Not many Christmas decorations have had songs written specifically about them, but the Christmas tree has been such a special part of the seasonal celebrations in Germany for so long that its virtues are extolled in a well-known carol, 'O Tannenbaum'. As the custom of having a tree as the focus of the Christmas decorations spread to other countries, so the carol has been translated into different languages. The tree is only part of the decorations, though, and there are many other items traditionally associated with the Christmas season, such as bells, crackers, baubles, candles and ribbons.

At Christmas it is easy to find attractive ribbons in seasonal colours – look in haberdashers' and cake decorators' shops. This simple mat was made by weaving together plain and patterned ribbons of several different widths. Work on a cork board and pin the ribbons in place as you weave them; finish off the edges with a border of plain ribbon.

Although Christmas trees are relatively new additions to the Christmas festivities in Britain and America, they have been part of Germany's seasonal celebrations for many centuries. Legend has it that St Boniface, an Englishman who went over to Germany as an early missionary, gave the German people an alternative to their pagan custom of worshipping an oak tree dedicated to the god Thor; instead, he encouraged them to use an evergreen fir tree in their midwinter celebrations to act as a reminder of new life through Jesus.

The custom of the Christmas tree spread through northern Europe from Germany; perhaps it was taken up especially quickly because there is a plentiful supply of fir trees in that region! In Norway it is still traditional today to sing carols while dancing round the Christmas tree, and often while dancing through the rest of the house too. It was German emigrants to the United States who took the custom across to northern America, and trees became common there in the early nineteenth century.

The custom didn't reach England until Prince Albert, Queen Victoria's German husband, homesick for the trees of his fatherland, introduced them at the Christmas gathering at Windsor in 1841. A print reproduced in the early 1840s showed Victoria and Albert with their children gathered around a splendidly decorated tree, and this was responsible for the almost immediate adoption of the custom by all the English families who could afford it. Prints from the nineteenth century show Christmas trees in England and America decorated with many of the items still available as decorations today: baubles, miniature stockings, tiny musical instruments, exotic birds, little baskets and paper cones full of sweets. In addition the trees of the last century featured decorated elephants and miniature furniture.

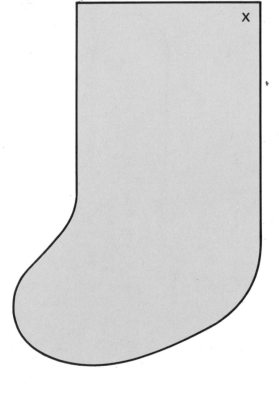

Tiny stocking shapes are used here as pot pourri sachets; they could hang on the tree, or would make an inexpensive present. Use two pieces of Christmas fabric, right sides together, and draw round the edge of the pattern shape; stitch round the line (apart from the top), then cut close to it with pinking shears. Turn the shape right side out, stuff with pot pourri or lavender, then turn the top edges in and oversew them. Finish off the sachets with bands of trimming and a loop of toning satin ribbon, adding a bow at the back if you wish.

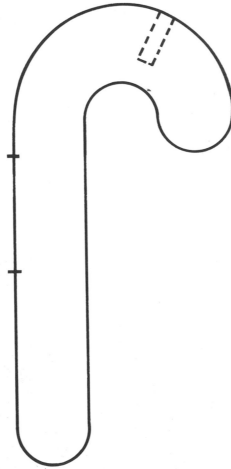

Old-fashioned candy sticks like these make pretty tree decorations. Use double-sided fusible web to attach narrow satin ribbon onto white felt in diagonal stripes. Lay the patterned felt face up on a layer of plain white felt. Trace the candy stick shape onto paper and pin the shape onto the front of the felt layers; cut ½in (1cm) extra all round the shape.

Insert a loop of silver ribbon between the shapes where marked, then stitch round the edges of the paper shape, leaving a small gap. Unpin the pattern, stuff the cane lightly, then close the seam with back stitches. Decorate each cane with a green ribbon bow.

Decorations for the tree vary from country to country. In the United States it is still common to use strings of popcorn – one of the cheapest and most readily available materials when trees first became popular – and also ribbon bows, a custom which is spreading from America to other countries. In Holland, Scandinavia and Germany, Christmas cookies are often made to decorate the tree as well as for guests to eat when they call in over the holiday period. Spain and Italy both have a kind of nougat, known as *turron* or *torrone*, which is cut into squares and then wrapped in paper and tied on the tree. In some European countries gilded nuts and fruits, also readily available materials, are common, and in northern and eastern Europe decorations made from straw are favoured. Blown glass baubles continue to be produced in more affluent countries, though these are tending to be replaced by less fragile plastic versions.

Most countries have candles as an integral part of their festivities. Martin Luther introduced the idea of candles on the Christmas tree, though these have largely been replaced by safer fairy lights. However, candles are still popular in other types of decoration. Advent wreaths contain four candles, one to be lit on each Sunday in Advent (the month before Christmas); sometimes carols are sung while each candle burns. In Italy, some houses have a giant Christmas candle known as the *ceppo*, which burns throughout the holiday season, and in Greece it is common to put a lighted candle on the grave of a dead relative at the midnight service.

Crackers are great Christmas favourites in some countries, though virtually unknown in others. The first cracker was produced by Tom Smith, a British confectioner, in the early nineteenth century. He wanted a novelty to promote his packs of bonbons at Christmas time, and hit on the idea of treating a strip of paper chemically so that it would make a small explosion when pulled in two. His idea was an immediate success, and became even more popular when he began to put paper hats and small trinkets as well as the traditional riddle or motto into the package – elements which still feature in crackers today.

These exotic crackers are made from yellow, white and gold crepe paper; if you can get decorated crepe paper like the gold-and-white starry version here, it looks particularly attractive. Make each cracker from two layers of paper; cut the outer one slightly shorter than the full length of the cracker, and trim its edges into points if you wish.

Use cardboard tubes for the bodies of the crackers; if you want to use them as real crackers rather than purely for decoration, fill the tubes with jokes, hats, trinkets and snaps before you add the paper. Roll the two layers of paper around the tubes, securing with a few small dabs of glue. Pull a piece of string tight around the ends to crimp them, then decorate with baubles and bows.

These effective cards are made very simply, using pre-cut card blanks which you can buy from craft shops. Slip bits of fabric or Christmas paper behind the apertures in the cards, then decorate them further with sequins, ribbons and bows, or shapes made in glitter glue.

Christmas trees make good shapes for Christmas crafts of all kinds. Very simple outlines can be turned into shapes for printing onto wrapping paper and cards, or used as guides for making decorated cookies, present labels, cardboard models or iced motifs. More complex shapes can be embroidered, or reproduced in collage, mosaic or paper sculpture, then embellished with foil, tiny baubles, ribbon bows or greenery.

The shapes of many popular decorations, such as crackers and baubles, are also easy to copy in different media. Look in Christmas copies of glossy magazines for inspiration, and you may well find that you can produce your own home-grown versions of expensive designer decorations! Simple shapes such as bells and candles can be used for both three-dimensional models in techniques such as papier mâché and clay modelling, and as outlines for two-dimensional designs in coloured paper, card, foil and fabric. Little decorative touches come into their own on trees and their ornaments; make full use of sequins, glitter glue, ribbons, beads and small baubles, tinsel and lametta, and gold- and silver-sprayed seeds, dried flowers and imitation fruits.

Make your own miniature tree based on a polystyrene cone. Buy a cone of the right height (from craft shops and from some florists and garden centres), then wrap a string of twisted tiny baubles around it in a spiral. Between the bauble string, fill up all the exposed pieces of polystyrene with dried flowers, seed-heads, real or fake foliage — anything which looks attractive — securing them unobtrusively with pins. Remove the baubles, then spray all the other items with a silver or gold spray; make sure that you spray from all directions so that all sides of the decorations are covered. When the paint is dry, wind the baubles into place again and secure with pins; top the tree with a star or other decoration sprayed the same colour.

15

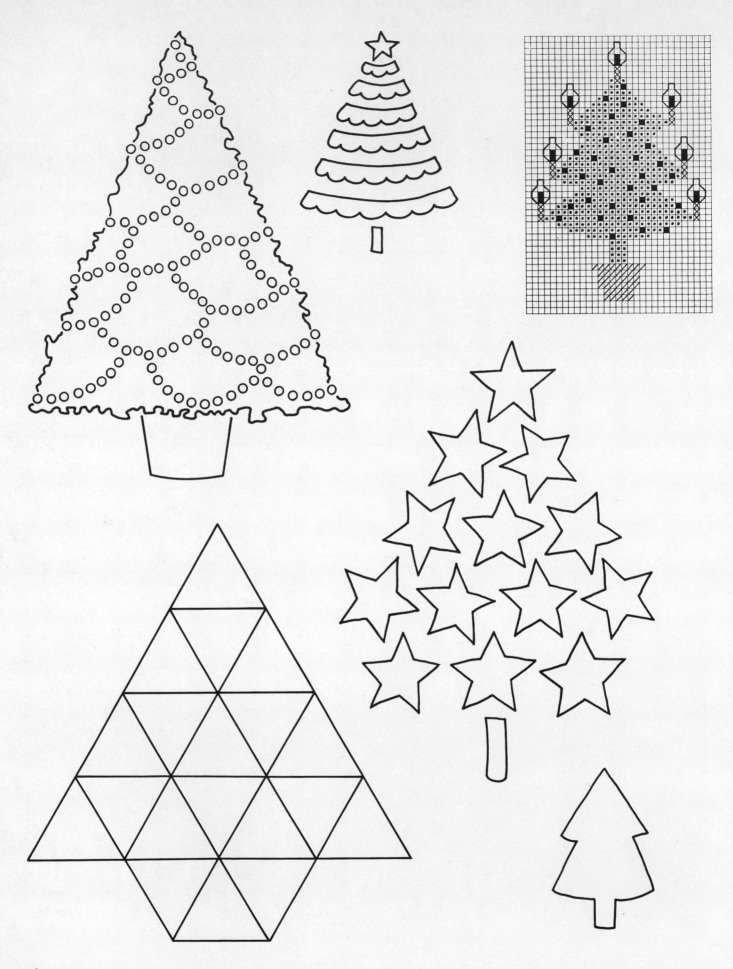

These pages focus on the Christmas tree itself and its decorations. As you can see, Christmas trees come in all shapes and sizes, and can be used for just about any Christmas craft. The simplest shapes are easy enough for potato prints or stencils for wrapping paper, advent calendars, table linen and cards, and can also be cut from fabric for appliqué. The tree based on triangles, opposite, can be made in stitched patchwork, either flat or padded, as a wall-hanging, while the charted tree could be worked in cross-stitch in the corner of a festive place-mat.

Trees made from a combination of materials look very striking; the realistic tree, top left, could be cut from felt or green paper, then decorated with baubles in glitter glue, or with actual strings of beads. The star tree can be made at any size, using tiny stick-on stars or large ones cut from foil. The bauble and candle designs can all be interpreted in coloured card or felt with glitter for gift tags or place settings.

Most of the tree shapes are easy to interpret in icing or marzipan, too, and the simple outline could be used for Christmas cookies or gingerbread.

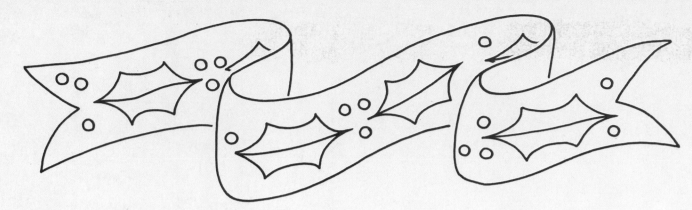

Trees are only part of the decorations at Christmas time; other popular types, such as ribbons and bows, bells, paperchains and crackers, are shown here.

The ribbon banner at the top is a simple shape for a giant card or fabric party banner; you could add your own Christmas greeting or a name in place of some of the holly. This design also works well at a smaller size, perhaps as a cut-out label for a present.

The stencil bow on the right is an easy but pretty shape to enlarge and then spray or paint around the edge of a tablecloth. The full bow below the stencil bow doesn't need to be actually tied; you could cut the shape from a Christmas print fabric, then pad it slightly with thin wadding and stitch around the edges by machine. Use it as a decoration for your wall, door or mantelpiece. The smaller bows can be drawn in poster paint, fabric paint, felt pen or glitter glue, and added as borders on cards and table linen.

Crackers are very satisfying shapes. For the cracker designs here, you don't have to make three-dimensional versions. You can cut the basic shapes from card or paper, then decorate them with whatever you have to hand – doilies, metallic stars, real or fake greenery, papercuts, small baubles and large beads, lace and ribbon. As a decoration for a long wall, try making a string of bells or crackers in bright card.

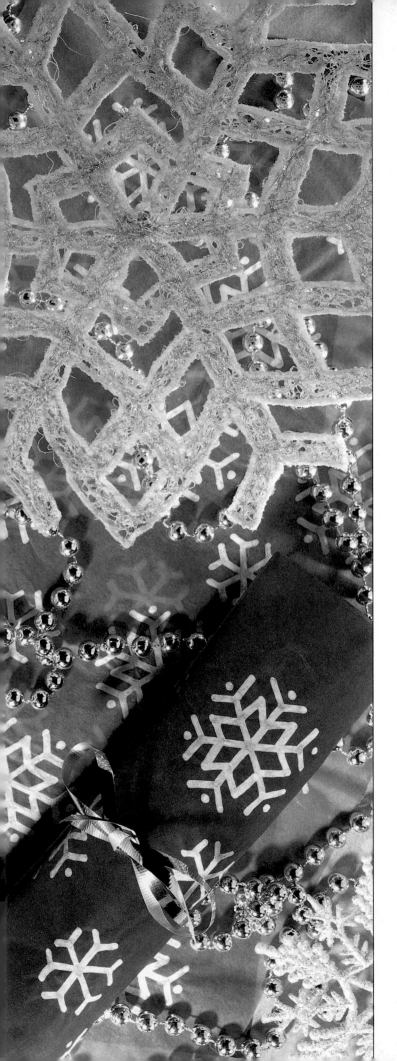

Chapter 2

WINTER SNOW

*The pure white softness of a big snowfall
lends its special magic to Christmas scenes
in the colder Northern countries. For some
lucky children, the pleasure of the season is
made complete by rushing outside to the
world of snowball fights, skating and
tobogganing, though they'll soon be back in
again for hats, gloves and scarves to
decorate the snowmen. Meanwhile, maybe
there's a piece of Christmas cake, the
white icing perfect for creating a snow
scene, to keep hunger pangs at bay.
Snowflakes themselves provide wonderful
inspiration for Christmas decorations,
their beautiful shapes giving us a more
permanent reminder of the fleeting pleasure
of a snowfall.*

Even though many of the people who celebrate Christmas live in countries where they never see snow, let alone snow at Christmas time, nevertheless snow scenes seem closely linked to our idealized image of Christmas. This is easy to explain in northern countries where snow is predictable at Christmas, but is less understandable in antipodean countries, where Christmas occurs in the midsummer heat! When one sees snowy scenes of Bethlehem, where snow is effectively unknown, things become even more confusing.

Part of the explanation lies in the early imagery associated with Christmas in Europe, the first continent to embrace Christianity. In the strongly seasonal countries of Europe, the festival comes in the middle of a long, cold winter, even if it doesn't actually snow. Also, there is strong evidence that winters were colder in earlier centuries, so Christmas snow would have been common then where it is a rarity now. In addition, ordinary people in earlier centuries had little or no understanding of the seasons and climate of other countries, and early carol-writers would have been likely to set songs about the Nativity in the frosty weather experienced in their homeland, just as some Italian painters of the Renaissance would naturally set their Nativity scenes in Tuscan landscapes with which they were familiar.

Snowman shapes are easy to make from icing – you have the great advantage that the medium starts off the right colour! This snowman is made from two circles of fondant icing, cut from flat pieces by using the edges of china bowls as patterns. Extra strips of icing are added for the arms, then hat, mittens, scarf and features are made from tiny amounts of fondant icing coloured with food colouring.

The tree is also made from coloured icing, but has been marbled by allowing streaks of the colouring to remain in the icing. Its decorations are silver dragées and tiny cake decorations, and dragées also form the snowman's row of buttons.

Another part of the explanation lies in the strong image of Christmas put across in nineteenth-century England by the Victorians, who popularized scenes of skating, snow-covered landscapes, snowy window-panes and other such views. They also loved sentimental depictions of beggar children outside in the snow contrasted with warm glowing scenes inside round the fireplace. Snowflakes themselves as symbols of Christmas can also be dated to the discoveries of the Victorian era, when science was a common leisure pursuit. During this era, the structure of snow crystals was first documented by using a microscope; their delicate patterns are too small to be seen by the naked eye. The beauty and impermanence of such tiny structures captured many people's imaginations.

It is cheap and easy to make your own Christmas wrapping paper, and you can achieve remarkable results, as these snowflake designs on jewel-like colours show. Buy packs of coloured tissue paper and draw snowflakes on them with opaque white felt pen (these can be obtained from good craft suppliers or stationery shops). Trace the designs here onto thick paper, then lay the tissue paper over and trace the lines gently with the white pen; don't rush, otherwise the pen will tear the delicate paper.

23

This cheery robin makes a very striking Christmas card. Trace or photocopy the design onto white paper, and colour in the robin and holly with poster paint, gouache or felt pen for a bright effect; go over the lines with a thick black felt pen (this is easier than painting them, and much quicker too). Mount the card in a specially bought card blank, or make your own by cutting a circular aperture in a piece of folded red card.

The symbolism of snow probably plays its part, too. Many people describe the first heavy snowfall of the year as magical. Outside, everything is different. The light and shadows are strange, noises are muffled, and everything is partly concealed. Old and ugly things look new and beautiful. Also, for many centuries the colour white has been used to denote purity, so it seems a fitting colour to be associated with the purity of the Virgin Mary and the Christ Child.

That friendly, cheerful-looking bird, the robin, is ever-popular in Christmas snow scenes. A legend grew up that robins got their red breasts because of their role in the first Christmas. Supposedly, Joseph had gone to find firewood, and had been away so long that the fire was in danger of going out. So that the baby Jesus wouldn't get cold, the robins, then ordinary brown birds, huddled around the fire and spread their wings over it to keep it burning, scorching their breasts in the process. As a result, their offspring have proudly been allowed to have red breasts ever since. A robin first appeared on a Christmas card in 1862, and the birds very soon became popular images; oddly, they were often depicted dead on Victorian cards, perhaps (like poor children huddled in the snow) to evoke feelings of pathos.

How Father Christmas came to be particularly associated with snow scenes, and to live at the North Pole, doesn't seem to be known. Certainly an English print dated 1879 shows a young girl posting a card addressed to St Claus, North Pole, so the idea has existed for well over a hundred years. As far as the people of Finland are concerned, a hill in Lapland called Korvantunturi is the true home of Father Christmas; as the area is populated by herds of reindeer, this seems entirely appropriate!

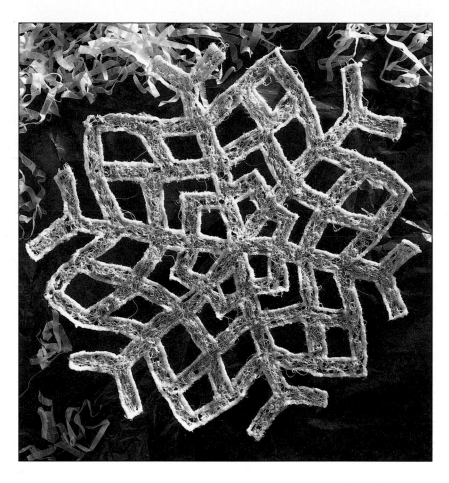

There are many ways of depicting snow in Christmas crafts. Cotton wool is an old favourite, and polystyrene beads (the kind that fill beanbags) or chippings (the sort that are used for packing) can also look very effective. White icing, of course, is excellent for snow scenes, snowmen, icicles and snowflakes, while whipped cream and meringue are other easy edible snows. For touches of snow on other decorations, try white or opalescent glitter. Opalescent and pearly fabric paints, too, make convincing snow on fabric and felt. Also, many shops at Christmas time sell fake snow sprays, which produce strings or layers of fluffy white plastic. Snowflakes can be difficult to draw; experiment by folding circles of paper into six segments and then cutting the segments into patterns with scissors or a craft knife – unfold, and, if you are lucky, you may have a good snowflake design.

Snowflakes come in many beautiful shapes, and can be used for delicate Christmas decorations. This one has been stitched by machine in white and opalescent thread onto cold-water dissolvable fabric; the fabric ground was dissolved away, then the snowflake was stiffened with dilute PVA medium so that it is firm enough to hang up without distorting.

Robins always seem to grace snow scenes, and there are many ways in which they can be used at Christmas. They are simple motifs to cut from paper, card or fabric, or you can stitch one from the chart onto, say, a napkin.

Snowmen come in all shapes and sizes; these two basic outlines can be adapted to suit you own taste. Use them for cards, cookies or tree decorations in oven-hardening modelling material. The mittens and gloves would make good label shapes.

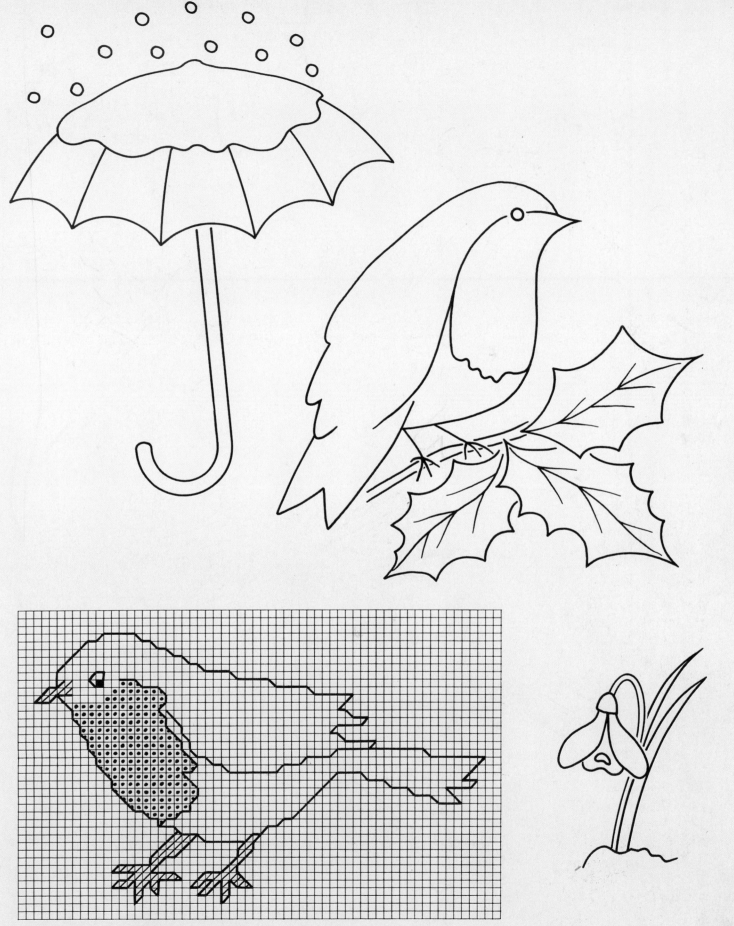

27

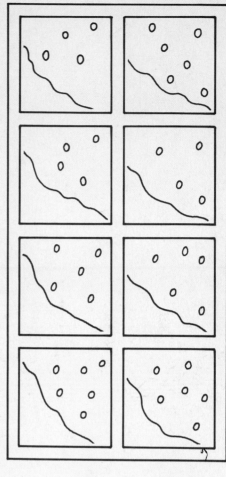

Snowflakes have endless possibilities for Christmas crafts. And, as we all know, no two crystals are alike, so here is a selection.

Small snowflakes make lovely decorations for cards, but they can be time-consuming to draw, so choose the simplest shapes, or use lino-printing or stencilling. If you spray glue through a stencil you can then scatter the surface with glitter to produce an extra-sparkly snowflake; or you could spray fake snow through a large stencil to decorate your windows. Silver sequins and beads, arranged in a regular pattern, make beautiful snowflakes on fabric.

Chapter 3

SHEPHERDS AND ANGELS

Sleepy shepherds on a bleak hillside at night would have been on the look-out for wolves and other predators. Nothing could have prepared them for the sight of a whole host of angels, telling them to go into the town of Bethlehem to find a special baby who had been born in a stable and was lying in a cattle trough! No nativity scene is complete without the shepherds with their sheep and, because they are simple shapes, they can easily be interpreted as three-dimensional models for a Christmas tableau. The angels, too, are central to the Christmas story and make beautiful decorations in paper, fabric or paint.

Shepherds have a special part to play in the Christmas story, because a group of ordinary shepherds were the first people to hear the good news that the baby Jesus had been born. They were told by the angels to go straight away to Bethlehem so that they could see the baby; he would be lying in a manger, which they would have found very strange, but when they went to the town, they found the scene just as the angels had described it. That must have been a story that they told for many years afterwards as they sat through the long nights, keeping watch over successive generations of lambs.

The Christmas cards and advent calendars which depict shepherds

The quaint pastoral scene here is made from oven-hardening modelling material. The shepherds are constructed from cones in purple and marbled yellow/brown (made by partially mixing two colours together), with sleeves added in the same colour. The heads are spheres of flesh-coloured modelling material, with beards, eyes and noses added in appropriate colours, and the head-dresses are made with flat circles in contrasting colours pressed to shape over the head and body. The sheep are made from rectangular cores of modelling material with black heads and simple legs; the wool was produced by extruding white modelling material through a garlic press!

After hardening, the shepherds' head-dresses were finished off with real twisted cords, then all the models were varnished to make them more durable.

arriving at the stable with lambs tucked under their arms may well be accurate. If the shepherds had been looking after newborn lambs, they wouldn't have dared leave them alone on a cold hillside at the mercy of wolves and other predators, so they would probably have tucked their lambs inside their cloaks as they went into the town. In some places in Europe, shepherds still bring a lamb to the church at Christmas for a blessing; this is an old ritual to ensure fertile flocks for the coming year, combined with a reminder of the shepherds at the first Christmas.

Shepherds are now integral figures in any nativity scene or play, and there are many ways of reproducing their straightforward outlines. On a small scale, a cardboard tube and a ping-pong ball are enough to provide a base for simple draped clothes for a model, while bent wire will make a crook. Alternatively, shepherds can be depicted very effectively in fabric collage or appliqué as part of a decorative Christmas frieze.

We love to show little woolly white lambs and bigger woolly white sheep on our Christmas scenes, but in fact sheep in Israel are quite dark and tend to look more like our western goats; however, they don't look quite so picturesque! You may well want to keep to the traditional way of representing white sheep and lambs in your Christmas crafts.

There are various ways of producing convincing-looking wool on your sheep. White fur, cotton wool and felt all give the right kind of texture, and you can make very effective cards and wall-hangings by appliquéing simple white felt shapes to a green background and adding black faces and legs. White and grey dolls' hair is appropriate, too, especially the curly kind which you can stick on with PVA or clear glue. White lace doilies cut into shapes make interesting fleeces, and some pasta shapes make very tactile sheep. Icing, salt dough, modelling clay and similar squidgy materials can be pressed through sieves, wrung through mincers or spaghetti-making machines and forced through garlic presses or potato ricers to make very realistic-looking shaggy coats.

The angelic figures here, perfect for the top of a Christmas tree, are based on flattened cones of gold card, covered with white doilies. Card arms, faces and wings have been added to the basic flat shape, and curly doll's hair (complete with bows) and painted features provide the finishing touches.

As for the angels who brought the good news to the shepherds, you will find many references to give you ideas, ranging from little Victorian children with wings to full-grown archangels. If you want extra inspiration, it is fascinating to walk around a graveyard and look at the tombstones from the nineteenth century. The Victorians loved angels, little cherubs and putti as well as 'adult' ones, and you will find some wonderfully decorative examples.

White and gold are the traditional colours for angels, probably because they are the colours which represent both purity and heaven. At Nuremberg in Germany there is a special Christmas market, one of the biggest of the country's traditional seasonal markets, devoted to selling the *Rauschgold Engel*, the ornate golden angels for the tops of Christmas trees. There is no doubt that angels look rather odd in dark colours, but silver is a good alternative, perhaps with pastel colours added if you want some variation.

This more stately angel, or maybe archangel, can be made to carry your own Christmas greeting on his banner. Cut a stencil by tracing and enlarging the shape onto thin card, then cutting out all the portions that are white; use a craft knife on a cutting board to do this safely.

Lay the stencil flat on a piece of thick blue card. Note that one of the angel's eyes and the stars on his halo are not linked to the rest of the outline, and should be positioned separately. Then spray or paint through carefully with white paint, making sure that the paint doesn't seep under the edges of the shapes. Remove the stencil in one clean movement, then leave the design to dry. When it is fully dry, cut about ½in (1cm) around the edges of the design; add a hole for a hanging string if you wish, or fix a hanging thread to the back with a hot glue gun.

35

Shepherds and sheep are essential to any nativity scene. Simple shepherd shapes can easily be interpreted as models in any size. For the naïve figure opposite, use a toilet roll inner or a cone of card for the body (in the same way as for the kings on page 70) and a ping-pong ball or cotton ball for the head; then dress the figure in simple clothes cut from paper or felt. The larger figures could be reproduced life-size as a dramatic painted tableau or smaller as a collage, using old scraps of fabric.

The sheep designs vary from realistic ones to silhouettes, and could be made up as simple models or cut from felt or fur fabric. The little charted lamb would make an unusual cross-stitch card.

On these pages you'll find your very own chorus of angels. Use the silhouette angel to make paperchains from folded white paper, cutting it so that the angels join at the wing-tips. The angel in the clouds, opposite, could be used as a Christmas card design, or large as a wall decoration, with your own greeting written into the space on the banner.

39

Chapter 4

FESTIVE EVERGREENS

A universal symbol of Christmas, the dark green leaves and blood-red berries of the holly provide a favourite Christmas colour scheme. The simple shapes of holly can be adapted to virtually every Christmas craft, from fabric-painted details on table linen to fondant icing shapes on a Christmas yule log. Other types of foliage have their place among the decorations, too: yew branches and ivy are useful evergreens which add colour while also looking decorative, and the blazing red of the poinsettia contrasts with the pure white of the Christmas rose.

Holly is probably the most widely used Christmas motif; it can be found on everything from paper table napkins to seasonal food and jewellery. The lush green of the holly's leaves and the bright red of its berries have come to symbolize Christmas in many countries, and the red and green colour scheme is inextricably linked with the festive season.

Evergreens of all kinds were used in many pre-Christian midwinter celebrations. Bay and laurel have been associated with power and victory since ancient Roman times, and ivy was thought to protect people against drunkenness – it is often found in pagan scenes of bacchanalian revels.

Mistletoe is an ancient symbol of fertility, and rosemary's meaning in the language of flowers is remembrance, so it was an appropriate plant for traditional annual ceremonies.

Because so many of these plants stay green throughout the cold, hard days of winter, they have always been considered symbolic of life in the midst of death, hope in the midst of despair, a promise of spring and new life in the midst of hardship. It was for this reason that, when Christianity arrived in the countries which celebrated midwinter festivals, it was appropriate for the churches to use the evergreens as symbols of the new life that Christ brought. The early church in many

What could be more festive than this Christmas wreath made from fresh holly and silk poinsettia flowers. Cut the holly just before you want to use it, so that it will be really fresh, and soak a florist's ring of oasis in water so that the holly will have moisture. Work your way around the ring, inserting the holly sprigs and distributing the berried portions evenly; if your holly does not have many berries, cheat a little by adding some sprays of artificial ones. When the ring is completely covered with holly, insert some silk poinsettia flowers at intervals among the foliage.

LEFT *Personalize a Christmas greeting with an exotic initial painted with a dry brush just dipped in gold paint. Add a sprig of quilted holly leaves (made by machine-stitching around padded shapes, then cutting out close to the edges), and complete with some bauble berries.*
BELOW *Glitter glue was used to create this all-over pattern of holly leaves and berries in a matching foil frame. To get the points of the holly leaves sharp, draw them out with the tip of a cocktail stick.*

countries used the holly as particularly symbolic of Jesus; as the carols tell us, the white flowers represent Jesus' purity, the red berries are the drops of his blood when he was crucified, and the green leaves show the new life he brings. In Scandinavia, holly is known as the Christ-thorn. However, to this day, mistletoe is banned in many churches because of its associations with the fertility rites of the Druids.

In Papua New Guinea, children decorate the churches with palm branches on Christmas Eve, ready for the Christmas Day services. In Mexico, bright red poinsettias are used for the *posadas*, or 'lodgings' – parties from house to house that commemorate Joseph and Mary searching for somewhere to stay in Bethlehem. Not many flowers are at their best at Christmas time, and many other countries have adopted the scarlet poinsettia as an appropriate seasonal motif.

Holly and ivy shapes are very simple, and so are easy to use in all kinds of crafts for Christmas. They can be cut from paper, foil and felt; made from clay, marzipan and papier mâché; piped in icing; drawn in felt pen and glitter glue; painted in poster paint, fabric paint, crayon and food colouring. You will get inspiration for foliage designs on every kind of seasonal item from carrier bags to marzipan shapes, and you may be able to find ribbon decorated with holly leaves and wrapping foil embossed with evergreens.

Single holly or ivy leaves are perfect for labels, printed cards, simple stencils, Christmas cookies and tree decorations, or they can be cut from coloured marzipan and fondant icing to decorate a Christmas cake or yule log. Make up small sprays of foliage, real or artificial, to decorate candle-holders, napkin rings and parcels – but do remember to play safe if you are using paper or dried foliage decorations around burning candles: never let the candles burn down so low that they might set fire to the decorations.

On a larger scale, holly and ivy bound onto a wire frame with four large candles would make a traditional advent wreath. Lavish swags of greenery make wonderful decorations for mantelpieces or festive tablecloths, while three-dimensional wall and door wreaths can be made from fresh or dried foliage, foil shapes, paper sculpture or salt dough modelling.

Foil holly, ivy and mistletoe leaves have been used to create this simple wreath. Use an oasis or twisted twig ring-shaped wreath base, then cut leaf shapes from foil which is gold on one side and green on the other – or use pre-cut leaf shapes if you can obtain them from craft suppliers. Position white candles at even intervals, and dot small coloured baubles around the wreath, securing them with wire twists or with dabs from a hot glue gun.

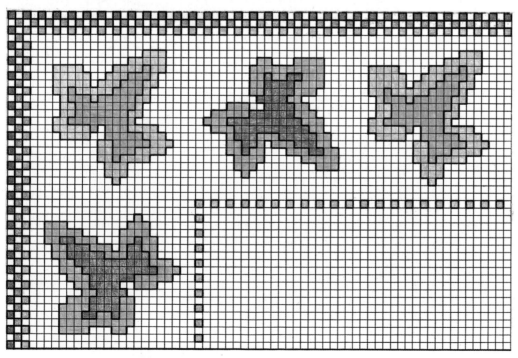

A cross-stitch border of ivy leaves gives a pretty foliage effect to this place setting, comprising a table-mat, coaster and napkin ring. You will be able to make all three pieces from a piece of 16-count cream Aida measuring 22 × 10in (56 × 25cm); cut a rectangle 16 × 10in (40 × 25cm) for the place-mat, 6in(15cm) square for the coaster, and 6 × 4in (15 × 10cm) for the napkin ring, then refer to the photograph to see how to arrange the leaves on the fabric pieces.

Wreaths, leaves and berries can be reproduced in just about any medium for Christmas crafts. The simple holly wreath opposite could be translated into gently padded felt shapes in shades of green; stitch the shapes over thin wadding by machine, then use the wreath as a wall decoration or table centrepiece.

Any of the shapes could be translated into icing decorations for a Christmas cake; the poinsettia would look particularly dramatic, outlined along the bracts and veins in red with a writing nozzle.

The simple holly and ivy stencil designs are perfect for the edge of a seasonal tablecloth, as are the charted holly-leaf motifs, translated into cross-stitch.

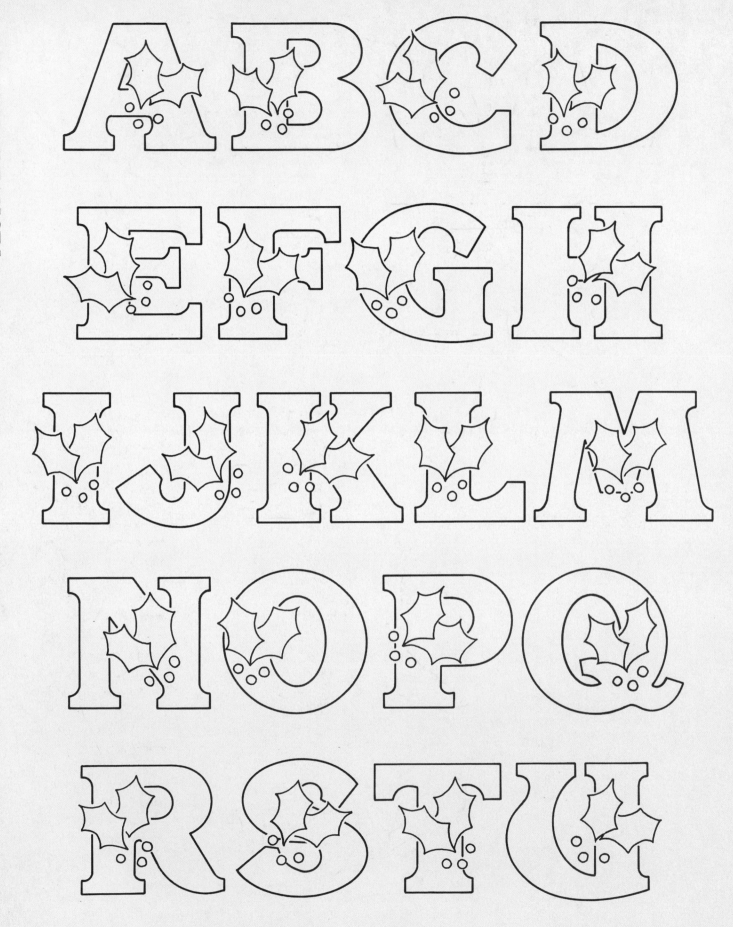

This simple holly alphabet has a hundred and one possible uses. First of all, you can use individual letters to personalize just about anything at the Christmas season. Try them cut from felt or embroidered onto individual Christmas stockings or cards. Alternatively, cut them from paper or foil to decorate cards, napkin rings or place-setting cards for Christmas lunch. For the berries you could use beads or tiny baubles on a fabric background, or a dab of red glitter or glitter glue on a papercut card.

Put the letters together, and you can spell out any seasonal greeting from 'Merry Christmas' to 'The Party's Here'! If you want to occupy the children for a while, draw the outlines of the letters large and let them colour them in; for extra fun, put each letter on an individual piece of card and string them together on ribbon or cord.

For a unique Christmas card, you could use the letters to put together a Christmas message or draw up the numerals for the year; then have the design photocopied small onto cards at your local print shop, ready to colour in yourself. Or you could photocopy your design onto paper or card for labels or party invitations. Colour each one in red and green with gold letters.

Chapter 5

THE NATIVITY

Renaissance painters loved to paint Mary and the baby Jesus in marbled and gold-filled palaces, but of course the first Christmas wasn't like that at all. The familiar nativity scene, well-loved by generations of children, had far humbler surroundings. But, in spite of its simplicity, the hay-strewn stable, with the ox and the ass resting beside the manger, makes a homely setting for the new-born baby. The figures around the crib can easily be created from everyday materials for a Christmas tableau, or the scene can be portrayed in paint or fabric on cards, stage backdrops or wall hangings.

This crib set is easy enough to be made by children, but looks very effective. Use standard corks for the bases of the figures, and ¾in (2cm) cotton pulp balls for the heads. Cover the corks with strips of coloured paper or foil, then make matching sleeves with hands sticking out; paint the hands and faces pink. Decorate the figures with scraps of cloth and felt, pipe cleaners, little baubles, strips of ribbon and lace.

The focus of the Christmas celebrations is, of course, the amazing sequence of events that took place in Bethlehem almost two thousand years ago at the first Christmas. As well as the events recorded in the Gospels, several traditions and legends have grown up about the first Christmas night. Legend has it that the ox and ass that were in the stable when Jesus was born recognized their creator and knelt down; an ox and ass are still often seen in traditional nativity scenes. Legend also says that bees hum praises to the new baby at Christmas time, and that at midnight on Christmas Eve, animals can talk, but only good people can hear them!

Several of our Christmas traditions began with attempts to make the Christmas story real to ordinary people, rather than an event that only priests could understand. The idea of the crib was begun by St Francis of Assisi. In 1223, near Greccio in Italy, he set up the first crib scene, life-size and including a live ox and ass. Ever since then, cribs have been very popular in Italy and Spain in particular, and the custom has spread to other countries. In Italy, before Christmas, the shops are full of figures for the *presepio*, as they call the crib, and in Spain and Mexico figures for their *nacimiento* are often set in wider scenes of Belen, or Bethlehem. In Poland, Christmas cards and letters are sent with an *oplatek* in the envelope; these are bread wafers embossed with a nativity scene, and in some households

the Christmas blessing on the family takes place as the wafers are symbolically broken and shared.

The medieval mystery plays and mummers also evolved as a way of bringing the Christmas story to life in an entertaining and down-to-earth manner. In surviving scripts for early mystery plays, the figures are shown as ordinary people, with the shepherds as simple, earthy folk arguing about what they had just seen and whether or not to go to Bethlehem. Many carols were written to be sung as part of mystery or nativity plays, including 'The Coventry Carol' and the German carol 'Joseph Lieber'. The Christmastide play has gradually merged with the revels associated with Twelfth Night – which often involved women dressing up as men and vice versa, with some kind of Lord of Misrule – to produce the modern Christmas pantomime. Something much closer to the original survives in the tradition of school nativity plays, when grubby rascals are rehearsed, scrubbed and dressed up to reappear miraculously as the angel Gabriel or a worshipping shepherd, to the delight of their parents.

Stained glass gives a very rich effect. This large panel is made from paper stained glass; the coloured tissue papers used inside the black paper outlines look very like the real thing. This kind of panel works well in a window over the holiday season; during the day the light shines into the room through the panel, and at night the lights inside the house illuminate the panel for passers-by.

Silhouettes can look very dramatic, as this card shows. Trace the shape below onto thin white card, then cut carefully round the edges with sharp scissors or a scalpel to give a firm outline. Draw round the shape onto black card or paper, using a coloured crayon so that the marks show, and cut out carefully. Stick the silhouette onto a sheet of marbled paper, then mount the paper in a foil or card frame in a toning colour.

Christmas cards and advent calendars have mostly abandoned traditional nativity scenes in favour of popular snow scenes, Christmas puddings, humorous pictures and such like, but there are plenty of sources of inspiration for creating your own, more timeless, images. Try taking a look at some medieval and Renaissance paintings, or search out some stained glass windows of any era, and you will find many nativity scenes or depictions of the Madonna and Child. Other useful sources of authentic settings for a nativity scene include atlases, or books on geography, Bible history or archaeology, which may show scenes of past and present daily living in the Holy Land; much of the way of life hasn't changed at all through the centuries,

The shapes of ancient Bethlehem appear in this simple yet very dramatic card. Enlarge the diagram to the chosen size, extending the back to the same height as the front, then trace the lines onto fairly firm card. Colour in the shapes of the buildings and palm tree with felt pens or bright paints, then go around all the outlines with a thick-tipped gold felt pen. Using a scalpel, cut carefully round the outside edges of the gold lines bordering the skyline, taking care to stop when you come to the fold marks. Fold at the fold marks to make the card stand up.

especially in more rural areas. You can create two-dimensional nativity scenes with painting, collage or appliqué, and there are many ways of making simple models to create a three-dimensional scene. Try using paper sculpture, or models based on cardboard tubes; keep the figures simple, as they only need to be representative, without too many fussy details. Another method is to drape wire frameworks (also known as armatures) with hessian or calico dipped in PVA medium; arrange the drapes to form cloaks, shepherds' blankets and angels' robes, then paint the models when dry.

Salt dough and other types of modelling material all allow you to experiment with realistic models, but you can have fun producing naïve figures too; look at the crib models produced in parts of South America for inspiration on bright colours and simple shapes.

The silhouette stable scene below can be interpreted in different media; try it small as a papercut, or make it larger as a wall decoration, using paint or fabric. Young children could even fill the outlines with different pasta shapes glued to a card background. It is also suitable as a backdrop for your own crib figures; make it to an appropriate size and decorate it with straw, corrugated cardboard and textured card.

The annunciation scene opposite is a simplified version of a painting by Botticelli. This could be interpreted on a large scale as a wall-hanging in paint or fabric collage, or on a small scale as a line drawing for a card.

These pages focus on the central figures inside the stable at Bethlehem. The simple outlines of Mary, Joseph and the baby Jesus, opposite, can be treated as flat shapes with paint, fabric appliqué or cut paper, or made up as felt finger puppets. Three-dimensional, dressed models can be built up by draping fabric around simple conical bodies.

Ox and ass motifs are part of the nativity scene. The ox is charted for a cross-stitch design, but could be made in paint or collage, too. The triptych above is a perfect shape for an unusual folded card.

Chapter 6

STARS

Stars in all shapes and sizes abound at Christmas time. They twinkle at us on wrapping paper and cards, and in shop windows and street decorations. Star shapes lend themselves to two-dimensional cutouts and three-dimensional models. Their outlines can be used for all kinds of Christmas items from seasonal cookies to foil labels for presents, and, of course, they make beautiful decorations for the Christmas tree. Gold and silver are favourite colours, but other colours look good too, especially in metallic or foil materials that give them extra gleam.

Stars of all kinds appear on this collage, made from a variety of seasonal materials. Stars have been cut from magazines and wrapping papers and are used to cover the background, which has then been embellished by star-shaped sequins and beads, plus stars cut from fabric and foil and painted with glitter-glue. The final result is framed in gold mounting card to set off the gold in the collage.

Stars are central to the Christmas story. It was a large star that led the three wise men, or kings, to Bethlehem and then hovered over the stable where Jesus was born. Also, because we think of many of the events of Christmas happening late at night – for example, Mary and Joseph looking for somewhere to stay, or the angels appearing to the shepherds – we picture clear, starlit nights in the Holy Land.

Stars are important Christmas symbols in many countries. In Poland, Christmas Day is called *Gwiadzka*, which means 'Little Star', after the star of Bethlehem; one of the Christmas gift-bringers is called Mother Star, and they also have choirs of boys known as Star Singers, who parade carrying large cardboard stars lit by candles, and sing carols while collecting money for charity. In Finland, *Joulutortut* are special star-shaped pastries made only at Christmas time, and in several Eastern European countries the Christmas celebrations begin when the first star appears in the sky on Christmas Eve. When Martin Luther introduced the idea of candles at Christmas, it was to symbolize the starry heavens from which Jesus came when He was born.

Stars are wonderful shapes for Christmas decorations. They are attractive, come in numerous different forms and are very easy to reproduce in many different media; even small children can draw or cut out convincing star shapes. The simplest versions are excellent for appliqué, papercuts, stencils and easy potato prints, while more complex versions can be produced in paper sculpture, embroidery, patchwork, paper stained glass, collage, clay and papier mâché. A group of stars can be arranged to form a decorative pattern, either regular or random.

If you want your stars to shine, there are many different ways of applying a glint. One of the most obvious is by using metallic materials; try foil paper or card for cutouts and paper sculpture, or cut your star shapes from sequin waste or metallic fabric for appliqué. Embroider outlines and details by hand or machine using metallic threads, and add sequins or shiny beads. To embellish them further, decorate your stars with tiny baubles or strands of tinsel or lametta. If you are stencilling or painting stars, you can create the basic shape by spraying or painting clear glue, then scattering glitter across the surface and brushing off any excess. If you can obtain glitter glue, which is becoming very popular, this can be used to stick down shapes and make them sparkle simultaneously, and you can also use it in place of glittery paint for drawing.

If you are making star shapes out of matt materials such as papier mâché, dried flowers or seeds, or modelling clay, spray the finished decoration with gold, silver or copper spray, or paint it with metallic paint. These days you can buy metallic powder paints, which are very cheap and can be added to various media such as PVA, poster paint and transparent fabric paint. Metallic and opalescent fabric paints are excellent; they may be made from a fine metallic-looking paint, or may have pieces of glitter in them to make them sparkle. Use them to paint stars on table linen, T-shirts and sweatshirts, embroideries, fabric tree decorations and banners. Star-shaped sequins are available in many different colours, and add a seasonal feel to all kinds of decorations.

Silver and gold stars twinkle from this mobile, which is simple to make, but very effective. Cut a large, multi-pointed star from gold card for the top, and from this hang strings of smaller, five-pointed stars cut from gold card and backed with silver craft foil.

This lovely star would look perfect on the top of the tree; it is stitched in long-stitch on plastic canvas diamonds (available from needlecraft and craft shops). Multicoloured metallic yarn and blue coton perlé have been used for the coloured stitching, with gold metallic yarn used for the outside border and the long stitches radiating from the central points of each diamond. The five diamonds have then been stitched together invisibly with simple oversewing on the wrong side.

Stars are often in demand to crown the top of the Christmas tree, and lots of the individual star designs here would be suitable. The two five-pointed stars on the opposite page, with central spines to each point, would lend themselves very well to paper sculpture in foil or card, or you could cut a single or double star out of flat card and decorate it with pens, glitter and sequins to use as your tree's crown.

Most of the simple star shapes here can easily be reproduced as lino or potato prints for mass printing onto cards or wrapping paper. They also make very good shapes for present labels, cut from an assortment of coloured cards or foil papers.

You can use the star shapes as guides for cutting Christmas biscuits, or for motifs to decorate the Christmas cake. Cut the shapes out in paper to the required size, then place them onto the cake and pipe around them; or trace the stars onto greaseproof paper, pipe directly onto the paper, then stick the shapes onto the cake when they have hardened.

The charted star would look effective worked in cross-stitch onto a set of Christmas napkins, while the interwoven star shape opposite would make a striking stencil motif.

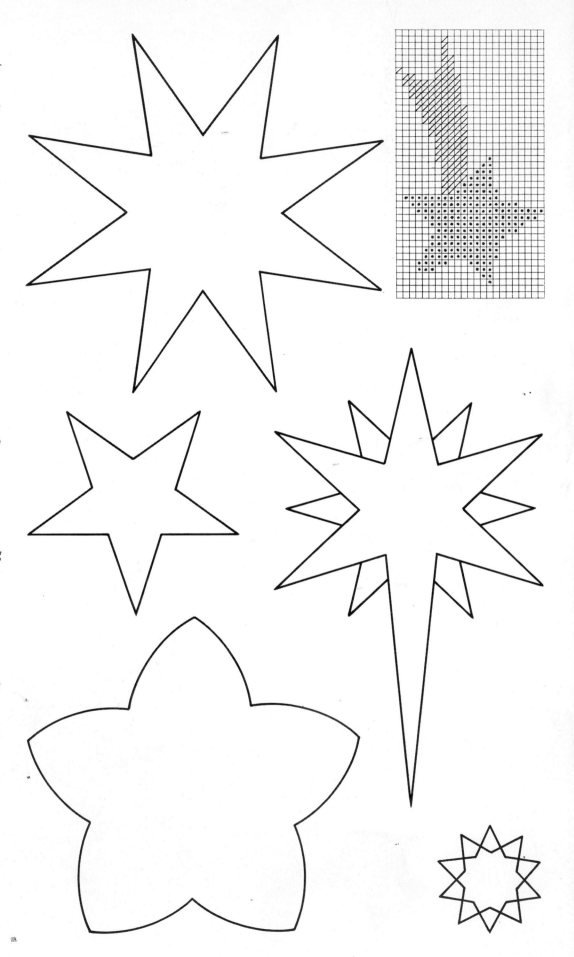

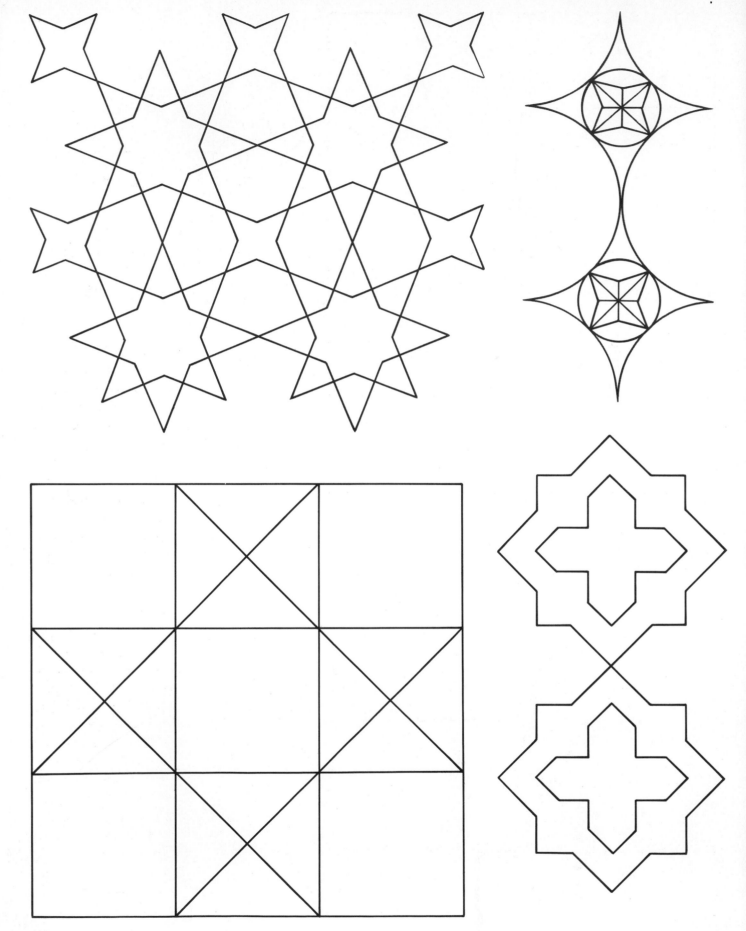

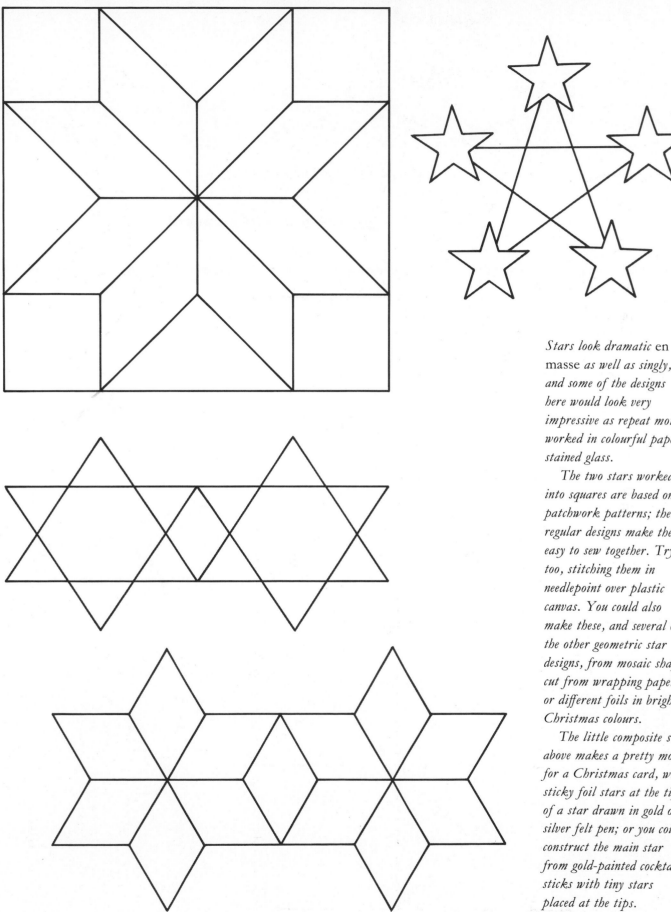

Stars look dramatic en masse as well as singly, and some of the designs here would look very impressive as repeat motifs worked in colourful paper stained glass.

The two stars worked into squares are based on patchwork patterns; their regular designs make them easy to sew together. Try, too, stitching them in needlepoint over plastic canvas. You could also make these, and several of the other geometric star designs, from mosaic shapes cut from wrapping papers or different foils in bright Christmas colours.

The little composite star above makes a pretty motif for a Christmas card, with sticky foil stars at the tips of a star drawn in gold or silver felt pen; or you could construct the main star from gold-painted cocktail sticks with tiny stars placed at the tips.

Chapter 7

THE THREE KINGS

There is a mystery about the three kings or wise men that fascinates us. Where did they come from? Were they really kings, or just wise men? How far had they followed the star, and for how long? And what strange gifts they brought to the baby Jesus! The contrast between the extravagant appearance of the wise men with their presents and the humble surroundings of Joseph's family could hardly have been greater. In our view of Christmas, the three kings represent everything that is mystical and opulent and, as such, make wonderful subjects to portray in rich fabrics, metallic papers, sequins and glitter.

The tradition of three kings visiting the baby Jesus is a long one, and modern nativity scenes often show three kings and three shepherds. However, nobody actually knows how many of them there were, and nobody knows whether they were kings or just important people. The account in the Bible simply says that wise men came from the East; they were obviously learned men because they had studied the ancient literature which told them that a star would show them the place where the King of the Jews would be born. They were also presumably people of influence, otherwise they would not have been able to afford the time or the money for the long journey, nor to bring the exotic presents that they did. In fact, the presents brought by the kings as offerings to the baby Jesus were the origin of our tradition of giving gifts to each other at Christmas.

The fact that the wise men brought three gifts – gold, frankincense and myrrh – has made people suppose that there were three of them, but it was Marco Polo who originally made known to the wider world a Persian tradition. When he was travelling through Persia (now Iran) in the thirteenth century, he reported finding the tombs of three kings, called Caspar or Gaspar, Melchior and Balthazar, who were venerated because they were the three who had visited Jesus. Persia in ancient times, and still at the time of Marco Polo, was a centre of learning in astronomy, and was also the cradle of the cult known as the Zoroastrians, who used gold, incense and myrrh in their ceremonies. A Christmas carol begins: 'Three kings from Persian lands afar . . . ', and certainly the concept of there being three kings has captured the public imagination.

These three cardboard kings give you the chance to use all those exotic trimmings you have lying around! Cut quarter-circles with a radius of 14in (35cm) from thin card, then cover them with coloured foil – a different colour for each king; cut out a segment at the top to fit the head, then stick the long edges together. Decorate the bodies with capes of metallic doilies and foil, chains of tiny baubles and large fake jewels. Make the heads from cotton pulp balls trimmed with doll's hair. Cut simple crown shapes from foil and decorate them, and make each king a present from a bauble, a tiny box or other trinket.

Some countries celebrate Epiphany, the feast of the arrival of the kings at Bethlehem, as the focus of their Christmas celebrations rather than December 25th; for them, Christmas Eve is January 5th and Christmas Day is January 6th. In one of these countries, Spain, children write their Christmas letters to one of the kings, usually Balthazar, rather than to Father Christmas, and on the eve of Epiphany they leave out a snack for the kings and some straw for their camels; in the morning, the kings will have left presents.

Different textures are the key to the success of this unusual card. Fold a large piece of black card into the concertina shape shown, then cut a further piece of black card to the shape below, adding a 1in (2.5cm) strip underneath. Cover the background and foreground of the card with lines of hills in fine, medium and course sandpapers, finishing off with sequin stars and a border of gold glitter. Stick the silhouette strip behind the final fold, then add a scroll cut from paper for your greeting.

Both Russia and Italy have a female figure which obviously stems from the same legend surrounding the kings; in Italy she is called La Bafana (from *Epifana*, Italian for Epiphany), and in Russia she is called Baboushka. The legend says that the kings or wise men met her on their way to Bethlehem; she decided to go with them, but wanted to finish sweeping her house out first. When she did finally make it to Bethlehem, she was too late; the Holy Family had gone.

In the Russian version of the legend, Baboushka took with her on her journey some black bread that she had baked for the baby, and put it in the

ABOVE *Oven-hardening modelling material was used for these exotic-looking tree decorations. Roll it out to $\frac{1}{4}$in (6mm) thick, then use the outlines opposite as templates to cut out shapes. Arrange plastic jewels in decorative patterns and press them into the modelling material slightly to leave impressions; remove the jewels and bake the modelling material. When it is cool, spray the shapes with metallic paint and attach the jewels with a hot glue gun. Add a loop of gold cord for hanging.*

RIGHT *Very simple tree or mantelpiece decorations can be produced by attaching foil-covered chocolate coins to a gold-coloured chain; use loops of gold cord secured to the coins with dabs of glue.*

empty manger before falling asleep exhausted. During the night she had a vision of the Baby Jesus, who was calling her to go with him, and she was found dead in the stable in the morning but with a happy look on her face. Russian children still sometimes find a piece of black bread wrapped in paper in the toe of their stocking on Christmas morning.

The characters of Baboushka and La Befana are usually depicted in brightly coloured traditional peasant costumes, and they often carry a broomstick. In Russia Baboushka is a kind of good witch, and uses her broomstick to ride through the air; she then comes down chimneys to leave presents by the hearth – a tradition which bears more than a passing resemblance to that of our Father Christmas.

In France Epiphany is celebrated as the *Fête des Rois*, the Feast of the Kings. Each family buys the flaky galette pastry with its hidden bean, which is sold with a paper foil crown; whoever finds the bean becomes king or queen for the rest of the day, and can wear the crown and order the family about.

Making Christmas crafts based on the three kings provides a wonderful opportunity for using all the opulent materials which can be found in abundance at this time of year. Sequins and sequin waste, glitter and glitter glue, glass and plastic jewels, metallic fabrics, threads and ribbons, foil paper and card – all of these come into their own for making models and pictures of the three kings. In crib scenes, the kings, with their lavish garments, make a good visual contrast to the simplicity of the central figures, the stable and the shepherds. In some countries which have elaborate crib scenes, it is the task of the children to move the kings a little nearer to the stable each day until they complete their journey to see the baby Jesus on January 6th.

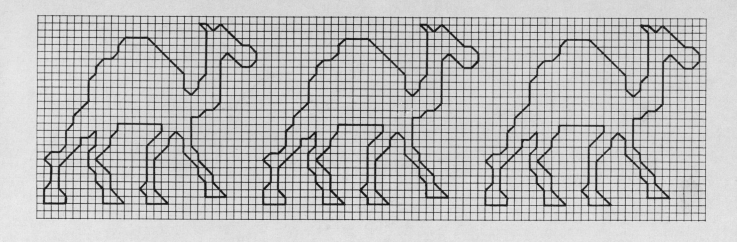

This is your chance to create decorations that glint and glimmer from every surface! The tableau of the three kings is a wonderful opportunity for a large wall-hanging. Try appliqué, using exotic fabrics with laces, beads and ribbons, or paper and foil with sequins and imitation jewels.

The kings' presents also offer exciting visual opportunities. Cover boxes and jugs with foil and decorate them with baubles, sequins and ribbons for nativity play props.

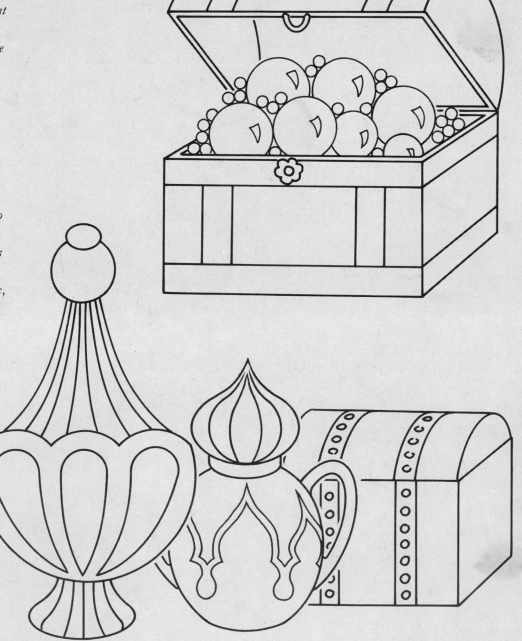

The designs on these pages give you a chance for even more opulence! Metallic foils, sprays, gift-wraps and fake jewels abound at Christmas, and you can make good use of them with some of the motifs shown here.

The fleur-de-lys motifs and other flourishes are associated with royalty, and look their best interpreted in gold, silver or copper. Paint the shapes onto parcels, labels and plain baubles for a lavish look. Or cut them from foil card and decorate them with glitter, glitter glue, sequins and fake jewels. Use the cut-out shapes as tree decorations or mobiles, or to decorate place-setting cards and napkin rings at the Christmas meal.

The stencil fleur-de-lys shape can be sprayed onto cards, party invitations and fabric; use a metallic spray on a rich-coloured background such as midnight blue, purple, scarlet, crimson or emerald green for the best effect.

The jewel shapes look very impressive made from scored foil card in different colours. Use them as tree decorations or along a mantelpiece, interspersed with gold or silver ribbon swags and bows. Try the crown shapes small on cards, or large as unusual wall decorations.

Chapter 8

TRADITIONAL FEASTS

For all of us, there are particular foods that we associate with Christmas. It might be warm mince pies, eaten on Christmas Eve with a mugful of mulled wine after a session of carol-singing, or a giant roast turkey on Christmas Day, complete with all the trimmings. Or perhaps it is traditional plum pudding, Christmas cake, or nuts and dried fruit which conjure up Christmas for you, or simply a bowl of tangerines, arranged with their green leaves in an old-fashioned fruit bowl. With a little imagination, festive fare can give you some unusual craft ideas.

In every country where Christmas is celebrated, some kind of feast is central to the festivities. Christmas has for centuries been seen as an excuse for an extra-special meal; even the poorest people would try to have something different to eat to single out the Christmas season and to break the monotony of many winter diets, when food was scarce and variety very limited. In some countries with an ancient tradition of Christianity, such as Greece and Russia, the feast may come at the end of a long meatless fast, sometimes as long as forty days, so the rich foods of the central meal are all the more welcome!

In addition, of course, the Christmas season is a traditional time for families to get together, so there are extra mouths to help eat dishes such as large joints of meat or exotic cakes.

The day on which the main Christmas meal is eaten varies from country to country. In some countries, Epiphany is still celebrated as the focal point of Christmastide, so people may have a large lunch or supper on January 6th. In other countries, Christmas Eve is the focus for the feasting; in Spain, the Christmas evening supper is known as the *Cena de Nochebuena*, or the Supper of the Good Night.

Glossy fake apples give a rich, warm glow to this decoration. Start with a straight plaited wreath base (you can buy these from florists' shops), and cover each end with wheat ears sprayed gold. Fill in the centre with fake apples in different sizes, interspersed with seed heads, and pine cones and florists' fungus sprayed gold. Finish off one end with a bow made from a wide ribbon with a colourful Christmas design.

Traditions associated with Christmas eating appear in slightly varying forms in different countries. Many cultures have some kind of tradition of setting an extra place, serving an extra portion or keeping some food by when the feasting is finished. Sometimes this is said to be in case the Holy Family calls in (so that they won't be turned away for lack of provision as they were in Bethlehem); sometimes it is said to be in case the Baby Jesus, or Christ as a grown man, wants to come and eat with the family. This may be the origin of the Western European idea of leaving a mince pie and glass of sherry out for Father Christmas.

Many Scandinavian and Eastern European countries traditionally have a pudding, soup or porridge made with grain or rice as part of the Christmas meal, often sweetened with dried fruit. In several cultures there is a bean or almond hidden somewhere in the mixture, and the lucky person who finds it is given special privileges, often taking on the role of king or queen of the household for the rest of the day, with the right to order other members of the family to do absurd things. The Christmas puddings of Britain and America started in a similar way; the pudding was originally a kind of sloppy porridge sweetened with dried fruit and nuts, served as a first course, and the silver sixpences or other charms traditionally hidden in puddings are similar to the idea of the bean or nut.

Sweet-filled cones were a feature on every Victorian Christmas tree, and you can use foil and lace to create your own versions. Cut 8in (20cm) diameter circles from foil paper, then fold the circles in half, foil side out, and snip a tiny half-circle away from the centre of the straight line. Fold each half-circle round your finger so that it overlaps to make a cone, and glue in place. Trim the tops with lace, then finish off with a narrow ribbon tied in a bow. Fill the cones with sweets.

Salt dough is the medium used for this fruit basket. Enlarge the pattern to the size you require [the example shown measures 14 × 10in (35 × 25cm)]. Roll some of the dough out flat and cut the shape of the basket; lay it on a large non-stick baking tray. Use the back of a fork to create the texture, and use twists of salt dough for the handle and edges.

Colour some of the salt dough orange and some green with food colouring or powder paint; use this to shape the tangerines and leaves. Bake the dough, then varnish it.

Some central parts of Western celebrations are relatively recent additions. Christmas cakes originated from the highly decorative Twelfth Cakes, confections produced specially for Twelfth Night, while sweet mince pies, as their name suggests, were originally made of shredded meat, seasoned with spices and sweetened with dried fruit. In pre-Cromwellian England, mince pies were made in a rectangular shape, based on the manger where Jesus lay in the stable; the tops were often decorated with a small pastry baby. When Oliver Cromwell banned the celebration of Christmas, he specifically banned eating mince pies, especially manger-shaped ones. The tradition was resurrected after Christmas celebrations had been reinstated, but people were still a little wary of making them in their traditional shape, and so made them round instead.

The other foods eaten during the Christmas feast vary enormously. Although nowadays the turkey is usually central to Christmas in many countries, this is a fairly recent introduction; in Victorian times in England it was still common to have roast beef or goose as the central joint, and several people writing at the time talked about the joys of blackbird pie at Christmas. Poorer people would join what were known as Goose Clubs, basically raffles where you bought a cheap ticket in the hope of winning a goose for your Christmas lunch; to avoid accusations of corruption, the draw was usually made by a small child. During the American gold rush, meats eaten as Christmas specials included partridges, grizzly bear, antelope, buffalo, elk, squirrel, prairie dog, mountain rat, swan, crane, quail, duck and oysters as well as turkey – basically, whatever was available. In some countries the main 'meat' is likely to be fish; the Russian Apostles' supper, their twelve-course traditional feast, features a large roast carp as the central dish. The important thing in all traditions is to have a good slap-up meal; what you eat may vary, but the central idea seems to be that it is as tasty as you can make it, and that there is plenty of it!

Food may seem an odd inspiration for crafts, but some shapes such as Christmas puddings are great fun to turn into different artefacts. Imagine Christmas pudding earrings made from oven-hardening modelling material, or a large felt advent calendar with appliquéd pudding shapes, one for each day. Use the gingerbread house design on page 86 for a large wall decoration made from coloured card, decorated with fake snow and perhaps real sweets, or create a table centre-piece from a pretty arrangement of Christmas cookies, each decorated with icing and a few jewel-bright fruit sweets. Look in cookery books for unusual seasonal recipes, and read about the traditional Christmas foods from other lands to expand your ideas for your own decorations – edible or otherwise.

Gingerbread shapes are a popular part of Christmas in many Scandinavian and other European countries; they are used both as edible treats and as decorations. Use any gingerbread recipe; if you want the shapes as decorations, add a little extra flour to make them firm rather than spongy, and leave the shapes to dry out for a few days after they are cooked. Decorate with lines, rosettes and lattices of royal icing, and press jewel-like sweets and cake decorations into some of the rosettes before they dry and become hard.

Christmas food lends itself to many interpretations in different materials. Try reducing the Christmas pudding motif in size to make raised badges or earrings in oven-hardening modelling material to wear on Christmas Day. For an unusual appliqué advent calendar, cut the pudding design out of dark fabric, topped by white felt icing, and stitch to the various pockets of the calendar; put sweets in most of the pockets and a coin in one or two. For fun, make some convincing mince pies out of salt dough as a centrepiece for a Christmas buffet table decoration; they will last from year to year! Garnish them with real sprigs of holly for a final flourish. Try something a little different for your Christmas cake by decorating the top with a dish of bright tangerines cut from coloured marzipan or fondant icing.

A gingerbread house makes a good alternative to the traditional Christmas cake. You can make one from real gingerbread shapes, embellished with icing and sweets, or a fake one based on coloured card. Follow the cookie designs to bake your own real cookies, or make salt dough shapes to be decorated and hung on the tree. The wrapped sweets and candy sticks, cut out from coloured foil, make attractive gift tags, while the charted Christmas pudding would look perfect in cross stitch on a table mat or card.

Chapter 9

SANTA CLAUS

There are various traditional gift-giving figures associated with the Christmas season. In some countries the gift-giver comes on St Nicholas' Day at the beginning of December, in others on Christmas Eve or Christmas Day; in still other countries, presents arrive on New Year's Eve, or Epiphany (January 6th). But more and more, all of these figures are being represented by the one jolly, red-cheeked grandfather figure known as Father Christmas or Santa Claus. The portly character of Santa conjures up excitement in children the world over, and his reindeer make humorous images for Christmas decorations of all kinds.

RIGHT This Santa figure is made from a plastic fizzy drink bottle with the top and bottom cut off. The head is a polystyrene foam ball covered in pink crepe paper, with black card eyes, cotton wool beard, moustache and hair, and a red crepe paper nose stuffed with cotton wool. Red crepe paper is used for his outfit, too, with details cut from black card and white felt. He has pink crepe paper hands. Finish off his belt with a real buckle if you have one to spare.

Santa Claus, or Father Christmas as he is known to many people, has his origins in a peculiar mixture of characters gleaned from many different cultures and traditions. In ancient mummers' plays, performed in mid-winter, there was often a Bacchus-like figure, a large jovial man with an overflowing cup of wine, crowned with holly at the centre of the merrymaking. In the pagan Yuletide celebrations in Scandinavia a goat was usually to be found as a central figure, and in Finland today their Father Christmas is known as *Joulupukki*, or Christmas goat. In fact, goats made of straw are still traditional Christmas decorations in some of these countries. But one of the most powerful influences on the formation of the modern Father Christmas was the figure known as St Nicholas.

Instead of keeping them in the box, put your Christmas chocolates in a custom-made sweet jar. Buy a plain glass container with a large mouth (so that hands can get in easily), and wash it carefully with detergent so that there are no greasy spots. Draw simple parcel shapes onto the glass with felt-tip pen, then paint in the coloured areas with glass paint, working on one side at a time with the jar lying flat so that the paint will not run. When all the paint is dry, go over the outlines with a black permanent felt-tip pen.

St Nicholas was a real person, a bishop in the fifth century, and, as with many ancient saints, various legends grew up around him. Many of these legends involved some kind of present-giving. One of the most popular involves three sisters, who were condemned to a life of spinsterhood because their father couldn't afford the dowry money for them to marry. St Nicholas supposedly threw three gold purses full of money through their open window (or down the chimney, in some versions), which landed in their stockings which were hung up to dry — or, in alternative versions, in their shoes! The link with the custom of hanging up a stocking or putting out clogs or shoes for Father Christmas to fill is obvious. In addition, St Nicholas became the patron saint of children, which strengthened the idea of him as a beneficent father figure.

The traditional Christmas gift-giver in some cultures is still St Nicholas. In Holland he is called Sinter Klaas, a corruption of his ordinary name, and is still dressed like a bishop, with robes, mitre and staff. He arrives by steamship, supposedly from Spain, and brings with him his assistant, Black Pete, who carries a large ledger listing children's names and whether they have been good or bad. Sinter Klaas rides round the country on his white horse, distributing presents to the good children, while Black Pete supposedly bundles up the bad ones in his sack to take them back to Spain. In Germany, sweets and maybe a few tiny presents are brought on St Nicholas' feast day by Sankt Nikolas, who is also known as Onkel Hans. At Christmas time, presents are thought to be brought by the *Christkindl*, or Christ-Child; in some versions this child is the young Jesus himself, while in others it is a fair-haired female child angel, dressed in gold and white with a crown of lighted candles.

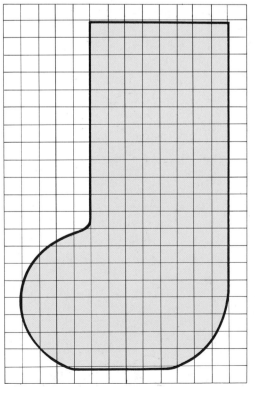

No-stitch appliqué has been used for these stockings. Enlarge the pattern as required. Cut the shapes out of double-sided quilted fabric; turn the tops over, then put two stocking fronts wrong sides together and bind the edges with a strip of bias Christmas fabric. Cut a series of individual motifs from the Christmas fabric. Attach them to the stocking fronts by putting a line of gold glitter fabric paint around the edges, so that it covers the raw edge of the motif and part of the fabric background; this will seal them securely.

Little purple foil-wrapped presents are incorporated into this table wreath to contrast with the traditional green and gold. A florist's flat cork disc has been used for the base; the candles are held in position with Blu-Tak (Fun Tac), then surrounded by fake holly foliage and gold holly-leaf shapes stuck into the cork. The foliage is set off by tiny purple foil-wrapped presents with gold cords, plus large and small satin bows, secured with glue.

In the United States a figure has developed called Kriss Kringle, who is a merging of several of these ideas! America was also responsible for the development of Father Christmas as we know him. In the seventeenth century, Dutch emigrants took the idea of St Nicholas to New York, where he began to undergo a transformation. By the beginning of the nineteenth century, he was fairly firmly established as the figure we recognize. In the poem 'The Night Before Christmas', written in 1822, he was a portly, jolly figure with red cheeks and nose, a white beard and twinkling eyes. It was this poem which began the popular conception that

Father Christmas, or Santa Claus (another corruption of the name St Nicholas), travels on a sleigh pulled by eight reindeer; it even gave their names. Father Christmas was unknown in Britain until the 1870s, when he suddenly crossed the Atlantic, was seized upon by the Victorian imagination and began to appear on Christmas cards, prints and cartoons galore. The Victorian Father Christmas generally smoked a briar pipe and was dressed in a suit that seemed to be made out of fur.

Father Christmas' main reason for existence is to bring presents to good children, and for years those presents have been traditionally-made toys.

Even in modern depictions of Father Christmas you don't see him with a sackful of computer games and space-age models; the perennial favourites are the ones which were seen in the Victorian celebrations of his visits: teddy bears, jack-in-the-boxes, spinning tops, trumpets, drums, soldiers, sledges, animals on wheels, train sets and dolls. The bright colours and shapes of the toys, as well as the traditional red-and-white colour scheme associated with Father Christmas himself, provide many opportunities for creating Christmas decorations and cards; the simple shapes also lend themselves to cut-outs and silhouettes, and it is not too difficult to make a small or large sledge out of cardboard, either painted or decorated with coloured paper, to hold presents or sweets.

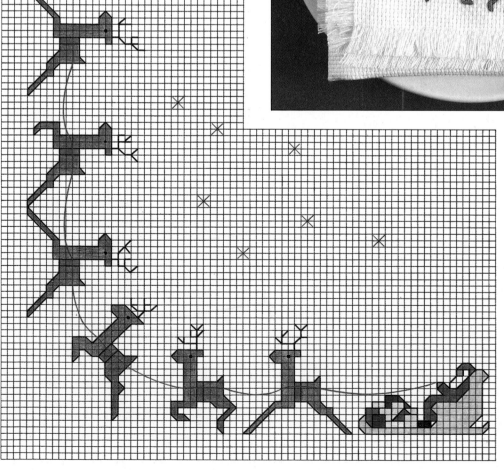

Father Christmas and his reindeer, travelling through the night skies, decorate the corner of a Christmas table-napkin. Work on 14-count aida, using two strands of stranded cotton and following the chart for the positions of the motifs; use double cross stitch for the stars, and outline the shapes in backstitch for extra definition.

93

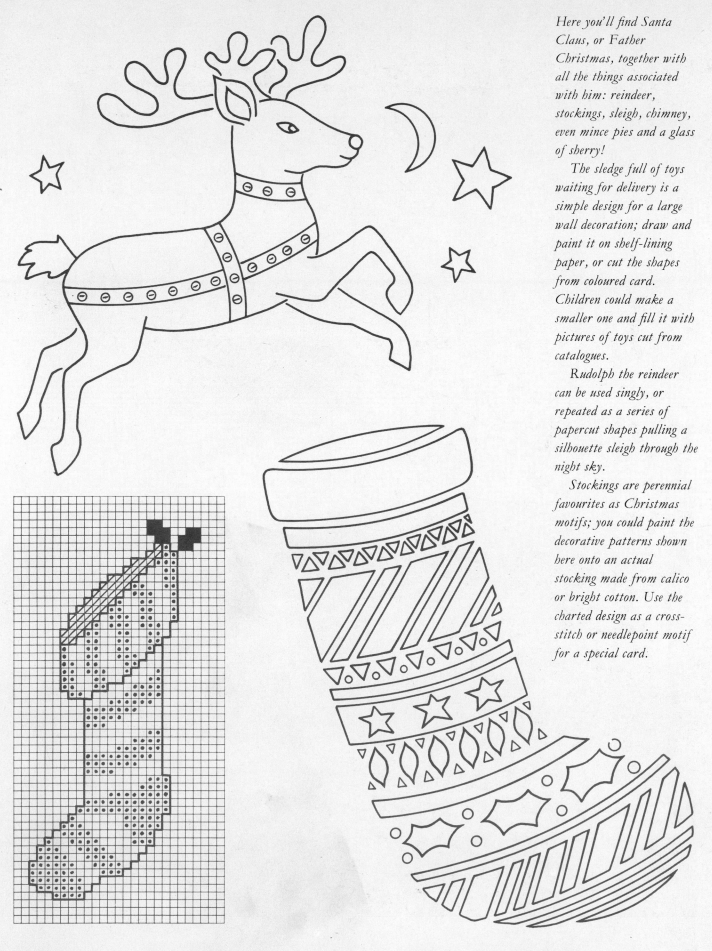

Here you'll find Santa Claus, or Father Christmas, together with all the things associated with him: reindeer, stockings, sleigh, chimney, even mince pies and a glass of sherry!

The sledge full of toys waiting for delivery is a simple design for a large wall decoration; draw and paint it on shelf-lining paper, or cut the shapes from coloured card. Children could make a smaller one and fill it with pictures of toys cut from catalogues.

Rudolph the reindeer can be used singly, or repeated as a series of papercut shapes pulling a silhouette sleigh through the night sky.

Stockings are perennial favourites as Christmas motifs; you could paint the decorative patterns shown here onto an actual stocking made from calico or bright cotton. Use the charted design as a cross-stitch or needlepoint motif for a special card.

95

These pages show the traditional contents of Santa's sack. Many of these motifs are basic enough for children to use as Christmas card designs, either drawn and coloured in, or cut from paper. The simplest shapes, such as the teddy bear or the presents, could be cut out and used as gift labels.

Toys allow plenty of scope for bright colours, and you could make a Christmas nursery collage which would still be appropriate all through the year. Cut the shapes from felt or other bright fabrics, and glue or stitch them to a plain background. For a slightly less durable frieze, cut the shapes from paper or card and stick them to shelf-lining paper.

Presents are simple shapes to stitch; work them on plastic canvas, then trim them with real ribbon as tree decorations, or embroider them free-style around the edge of a Christmas-tree skirt.

96

Chapter 10

A VICTORIAN CHRISTMAS

The Victorian idea of Christmas seems to epitomize everyone's image of a perfect traditional celebration. The house is decorated from top to toe with greenery and a giant Christmas tree is the centrepiece of the decorations, surrounded by a pile of exquisitely wrapped presents. The family is all together, sitting down to a great feast, with a gigantic, spherical, flaming plum pudding taking pride of place. Now it is time to pull the crackers and play silly games until later, when carols are sung around the piano. Traditional images of Christmas never lose their appeal, and make wonderful motifs for decorations.

The Victorian touch is captured in these little old-fashioned boot shapes, which you can fill with stuffing to go on the Christmas tree or use as little lavender or pot pourri sachets. Use the pattern to cut out pairs of boot shapes from felt, and oversew them together round all the edges except the top. Stuff gently, then oversew the top edge, and decorate with scraps of lace and tiny beads to look like buttons down the sides.

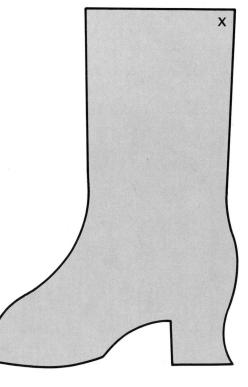

For Christmas symbols to decorate cards, calendars and Christmas trees, many people return to the era which epitomizes the traditional Christmas: Victorian England. Although at this time many children from poor families were made to work in often appalling circumstances from a very early age, Victorian art, which included Christmas art, celebrated the image of the plump, happy, innocent child, dimpled hands clutching an artless letter to Father Christmas as little eyelids drooped over rounded cheeks. Children pressed their noses up against square-paned shop windows, feasting on the sights of rocking horses and dolls, or candy sticks and humbugs, in the warmth inside. Angels, favourite motifs of Victorian times, were often depicted as little children with wings.

This unusual design for a round tablecloth would set off a Christmas buffet table perfectly; keep the old-fashioned feel by decorating the table with candles and fresh greenery. Divide your round tablecloth into equal segments and use the chart to enlarge and cut stencils for each of the colours: light green, dark green, pink and gold. For each stencil, only cut out the areas that appear in that colour.

First spray through the light green stencil around the edge of each segment. When this is dry, do the same with the dark green, the pink and the gold stencils. Spray a light spattering of green over the whole pattern area to give extra depth, then gather the edge of the cloth between the stencilled swags and finish with a gold bow.

A Victorian girl and her doll appear in this expressive silhouette; the design was inspired by a sketch that Queen Victoria made of her daughter Vicky in 1846. In the photograph you can see several very different ways in which you can use the silhouette to make unusual cards trimmed with doilies, bows and lace edgings; the shape itself is cut from thin black card or black paper.

Cards and prints looked back to more traditional, more attractive winter scenes than the factory chimneys that met many people's eyes outside their windows. Children and adults alike were shown enjoying wholesome traditional pursuits such as skating and tobogganing. Family groups walked through romantic snow-scenes to snow-covered churches, or sang carols in the snow by the soft light of hand-held lanterns. Picturesque stage-coaches carried top-hatted men and ladies with bonnets and muffs through the snow to a warm inn, where the cheery-faced innkeeper was ready to welcome them inside with piping hot drinks and good food.

The Victorians were responsible for establishing Christmas as western countries celebrate it. With their large families and often servants to feed as well, a vast amount of food was needed, and the turkey began to be popular as the central part of the feast; in those days turkeys could be bought weighing up to 40lb! These were also useful for some of the philanthropic exercises in which the Victorians excelled; many organizations such as churches and women's groups laid on meals for poor families or orphans, and cooking one large turkey was an economical way of feeding so many people well. The first official English Christmas card ever produced exemplified these different trends; it showed a family gathering in the centre, all drinking a toast, flanked by images of feeding the hungry and clothing the poor.

Christmas cards themselves were invented by the Victorians. The first one was produced by Henry Cole, a gallery owner, in 1843; it was designed by John Caldecott Horsley, and one thousand copies were printed by lithography, hand-coloured, and sold for the princely sum of one shilling. For the first few years after that, a minority of well-off families took up the idea and had their own Christmas cards printed, aided by the Penny Post which was introduced in 1840, and by the 1850s and 1860s the concept of cards had become quite popular. In the 1870s the Halfpenny Card Post was introduced, which brought the possibility of sending cards into the reach of many poorer families. The imagery on Victorian Christmas cards was not all that we might expect; the earliest cards often showed gauzily clad fairies, elves sitting on toadstools, water-babies, children playing on the beach and other kinds of designs not usually associated with the Christmas season.

Old-fashioned ribbons give a Victorian feel to a flower basket. Make the bows and swags from tubes of Christmas fabric, then dip them in fabric stiffener and mould them to the shapes you want, keeping folds in position with clothes pegs. Leave to dry, and the fabric will be permanently stiffened in the required shape.

Meanwhile, spray the basket red with car paint, making sure that you have sprayed into all the crevices. Cut a large circle of Christmas fabric and pleat and tuck it to fit the basket; secure all the fabric and ribbons in place with a hot glue gun.

Along with the introduction of the Christmas tree as the focus of the house decorations, the Victorians were responsible for the wholesale resurrection of the custom of decorating with greenery. For many paupers, the gathering and selling of holly, ivy, yew and fir trees provided a much-needed source of income during the hard winters. The Victorians also reinstated the concept of the Yule log, an ancient Scandinavian tradition; the Yule log was the biggest log that could be found, and traditionally had to burn without going out all through the Christmas festivities.

This was the era of the spherical plum pudding, too. The pudding had developed through the eighteenth century from a kind of porridge into a firmer pudding, and by the end of the nineteenth century giant versions were being produced which took several days to cook, and which were served crowned with holly sprigs and a halo of flaming brandy.

For a traditional feel to your Christmas crafts, try recreating some of the symbols of Victorian, or pre-Victorian, England. Stage-coaches, traditional lanterns and lamp-posts, crown glass windows covered in snow, Victorian ladies and gentlemen muffled up against the cold and singing carols under a lamp-post – all these look good on Christmas cards and wall decorations. Look at old prints and books for clothing details and inspiration. For an authentic look, keep the colours a little duller than today's traditional Christmas colours, with plenty of dark green foliage and real or imitation fruit, large ribbons and bows, and not too much foil and sparkle. For a traditional-looking alternative to your ordinary Christmas cake, create your own Yule log covered in chocolate and sprinkled with icing sugar 'snow'.

Découpage was a craft beloved by the Victorians; you can capture the essence of a Victorian Christmas by making your own découpage project. Collect Christmas cards or prints which are reprints of Victorian designs (some shops sell books of these designs specifically for découpage), and use them to cover a tin or box. When the découpage is complete, line the container with red or gold paper.

These simple stencil bows can be used in many different ways: as tree decorations, as individual decorations for pictures or mirrors, or along the mantelpiece. Enlarge the design from the graph and cut the stencil from thin card, then lay it on the top of a piece of coloured foil card and spray with spray glue. Remove the stencil and scatter coloured glitter over the glued areas. When the glue is dry, shake off any excess glitter and cut the shape out, leaving a border of card around the stencilled design.

A Victorian Christmas would not be complete without a walk to a snow-covered church for carol-singing. The church would add a traditional touch to a Christmas card design, and also makes a simple but unusual design for a cake; you could assemble the cake in the shape of the church, complete with white fondant icing for the snow, or just pipe in the outlines on a flat-surfaced cake.

Snow-covered window-panes are traditional in Victorian scenes; stitch the little charted design in cross-stitch onto dark aida fabric for an almost abstract card design. Work the bull's eye panes in backstitch. The stained glass window motif makes another effective card shape to fill as you wish.

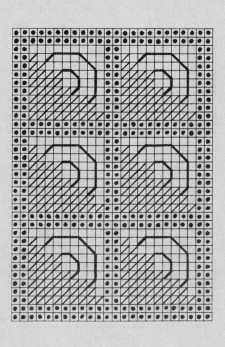

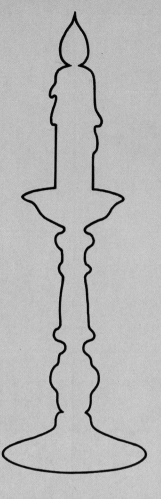

The Victorians loved to have a lavish spread at Christmas. The stencil of the fruit piled high in a decorative bowl would look beautiful on the corner of a white tablecloth for your own Christmas feast. Mix subtle colours of fabric paint and apply with a stencil brush for a softly shaded appearance. Add a touch of gold paint here and there to enhance the festive look.

The garlanded and beribboned mantelpiece with a cosy log fire would make a seasonal image for a Christmas card, while the candle motifs are perfect for gift tags.

Chapter 11

THE CHRISTMAS MESSAGE

'Glad tidings of great joy I bring to you and all mankind.' So said the angel that appeared to the shepherds, and throughout many parts of the world Christmas is known as the season of goodwill. It is a bright and cheerful respite in countries where winter is long and hard, and for everyone it provides an excuse for parties, get-togethers and outings. And, as the end of the year comes hard on the heels of Christmas itself, we look ahead to the promise of the New Year. That symbol of peace and hope, the dove, is shown in this chapter, with some beautiful lettering for your own personal greetings.

Felt doves hang from a ring of ivy to make a Christmas mobile. Cover one piece of white felt with strips of gold braid, then cut wing shapes out of this and fuse to the bodies; stitch the body pieces together, padding them slightly, and suspend from the ivy-covered ring.

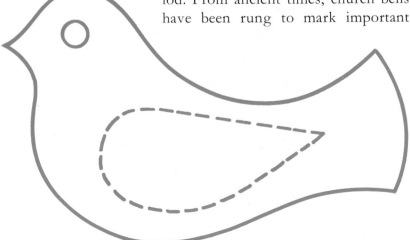

The message that the angels brought to the shepherds was for all mankind: that the Saviour of the World was born and that He had come to bring peace on earth and goodwill to all men. In Finland, the Christmas peace is proclaimed publicly from the Cathedral in Turku, a tradition that started in the Middle Ages; the Finns take this Christmas peace very seriously, and crimes are punished more severely if they are committed during the Christmas period. From ancient times, church bells have been rung to mark important events, and even in areas where the bells usually just mark the time, they are often rung in joyful peals on Christmas morning. It was this noise which woke Ebenezer Scrooge after his dreams in Charles Dickens' well-known fable, *A Christmas Carol*.

Each language has developed its own Christmas greetings, from a straightforward English 'Merry Christmas' to the Scandinavian '*Godjul*', which makes reference to the older Yuletide celebrations. Many countries, too, have their own unique Christmas celebrations and rituals. In Norway, and in households of Norwegian descent in other countries, families often sing and dance round the Christmas tree, and then run and dance, holding hands, round all the other rooms of the house. In Britain, many people still observe the custom of kissing under the mistletoe; if you are standing under the mistletoe sprig, you are fair game for anyone of the opposite sex to deliver a kiss on the cheek. To limit unwanted attentions, you are supposed to remove one of the berries from the mistletoe after each kiss; when all the berries have gone from the sprig, that signals an end to the kissing opportunities.

One tradition that has spread from its original source is the Christingle service, a special kind of Christmas family service that originated in Scandinavia. In a Christingle service, each child and adult is given an orange. The orange represents the world, and one half of it is wrapped in silver foil to represent the transformation of the world by Jesus' love. Around the divide is a red ribbon, which stands for Christ's blood, and in the centre is a lighted candle, showing that Jesus is the light of the world. Around the candle are placed four cocktail sticks decorated with fruit and nuts, which represent the many good things that God provides for us all.

TOP *Two simple dove outlines cut from foil make a striking greetings card. Cut the shapes from foil card using a craft knife, then mount them on a pale green foil background and frame them with darker green. Use a stick glue rather than clear glue, as clear glue marks foil very badly if it spreads.*

LEFT *A stylized dove outline has been used for this piece of machine embroidery, worked in a line of silver satin stitch over a background of ragged squares of translucent fabrics. Patches of metallic fabric paint in the background pick up the glint in the silver dove.*

The dove has come to be associated with peace and is now used worldwide as a symbol for the peace on earth that the angels promised. The beautiful shape of a dove provides excellent inspiration for Christmas crafts; imagine a large dove cut from silver card as a striking decoration on a dark-painted wall. Dove shapes are simple enough to be used as guides for decorating edible goodies such as Christmas cakes and tree cookies, and they make good outlines for appliqué as well as being ideal for printing onto cards, wrapping paper and labels. Doves in real life, and in most depictions of them, are white, which is another reason why they are used as a symbol of innocence and peace, but they can look very effective in silver and gold too.

Doves are becoming very popular Christmas motifs, representing the message of peace, and on these pages you'll find doves and olive branches in different styles. Many dove shapes are simple enough to be reproduced by stencilling or printing onto Christmas cards, and you could build up a design including the globe motifs.

For speed, try using a sharp scalpel or craft knife to cut several layers of thick paper at once; use the finished shapes to decorate cards or as present labels. A white dove would also be a good image for a New Year party invitation, when you might not want a specific Christmas motif.

If you like embroidery, you could stitch the charted dove as a little picture in needlepoint or cross stitch for an unusual present.

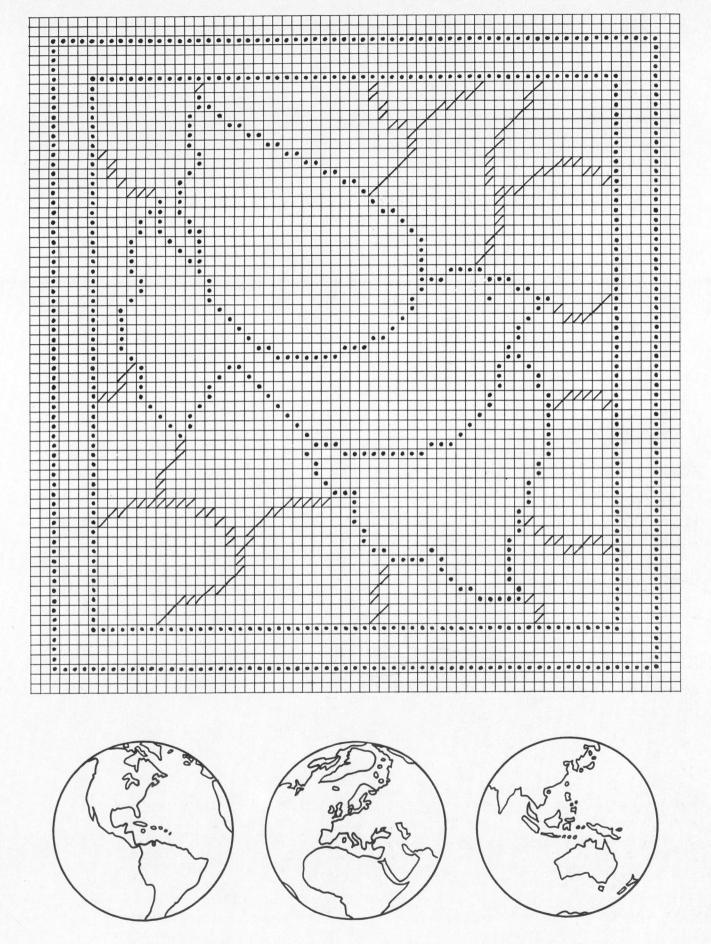

ABCDEFG
HIJKLMN
OPQRST
UVWXYZ
12345
67890

On these pages are alphabets and numerals in different styles. You'll find them very useful for all kinds of Christmas crafts. Try your hand at painting banners, or compose a personal greeting in Gothic script. If you have a steady hand, decorate a Christmas cake with piped greetings in different languages, or simply ice a large 'Noël' with the numerals for the year underneath. The letters also work well in embroidery which could be used on Christmas cards or to name a stocking.

ABCDE
FGHIJ
KLMNO
PQRST
UVWX
XYZ
1234567890

Chapter 12

CHRISTMAS CAROLS

From school carol concerts to carol-singing from house to house on Christmas Eve, you can't separate Christmas from music. Even pop stars bring out new records to try and hit that Christmas spirit, or sing their own versions of old favourites. Some families put on well-loved records of Christmas music as they decorate the tree or ice the cake, often seen as the real beginning of the Christmas festivities in the household. And increasingly in many countries, people gather for community carol-singing in the open air, making the most of the season of goodwill.

Singing is associated with Christmas even for the least religious amongst us, and virtually everyone enjoys a good carol service. The tradition of carol-singing is based on the example of the angels singing praises to God after they had told the shepherds about Jesus' birth, and goes back at least as far as the thirteenth century. Many Christmas depictions of angels show them singing – some even using carol-sheets, pre-sumably in case they forget the words! – or playing musical instruments.

Carols have traditionally been cheer-ful, joyful, rumbustious affairs; the word itself is related to older words meaning 'to dance in a ring', and some of the most ancient carols, such as 'Tomorrow Shall be My Dancing Day', echo this idea. In earlier centuries the carols were sung by priests and choirs from the churches, but, as time went on, the tradition broadened to take in the church congregations, and later anyone who wanted to join in as the groups went from house to house. The words and tunes of the most popular carols were passed down the genera-tions orally, or aurally, but after the invention of printing people began to make collections of carols on broad-sheets and in booklets. The oldest surviving fragments, dating from 1521, feature 'The Boar's Head Carol'. These later carol-singers would usually take a few instruments with them as they went round the village, to give their singing a lead and help them to keep in tune, unlike earlier unaccompanied church singers with more musical training.

These whimsical choirboys are made from double cones of paper, with flattened cones of white paper for the sleeves. The heads are ping-pong balls with wool hair and paper features glued on; the join between head and body is covered with a white crepe paper ruff. Each choirboy reads his own music – or comic!

Music is the theme for the decorations on this page; all the ideas use photocopies of music manuscripts.

LEFT *The tree decorations are made from rolled, twisted and pleated paper, decorated with red ribbons and gold treble clefs.*

BELOW *The tray is made from photocopies of music at different sizes, torn into random pieces and then used as the final layer in a papier mâché tray. The finished tray has been sprayed with several layers of glossy polyurethane varnish to give it a sheen and make it more durable.*

Many carol-singers in past generations either took around with them, or expected to be given, hot spiced wine or punch. The English mulled wine has its origin in the wassail cup, which was a drink of hot spiced wine or cider and apples; wassailers would travel from house to house and from orchard to orchard during early January, calling out 'Wassail' (or 'Be whole!') as a ritual to try and ensure that their fruit trees would be fertile and productive in the coming year. After a while the orchards were forgotten and the drinking went on; 'wassail' came to be a greeting meaning 'good health' to people who drank the wassail cup, and the custom and its associated songs were blended into the custom of carol-singing from house to house.

Cherub musicians play Christmas carols on this very pretty wreath. Two small plaster figures have been wired to an ordinary twig wreath base, then the whole decoration sprayed gold. A purple twisted paper bow was sprayed lightly with gold to give it an antiqued appearance, and purple star sequins at the top of the wreath complete the decoration.

Different countries in modern times have different carol-singing rituals. In Greece, it is customary for the children of the village or town to go singing around the neighbourhood; they are given cakes, nuts and small presents. In Norway carols are often sung around the tree, and in Germany around the lighting of the advent wreath, while other countries have developed outdoor carol-singing parades. In Australia over the past thirty or so years a custom has grown for large-scale outdoor community carol-singing; people gather round giant decorated Christmas trees in large public places such as town squares, and money is collected for charity.

Some carols are associated with legends and stories of Christmas time rather than with the central story of the Nativity. Some examples of these are 'Good King Wenceslas' (a carol based on a true story of a philanthropic king in eastern Europe), 'I Saw Three Ships Come Sailing In', and 'The Twelve Days of Christmas'. Other carols are glorified drinking songs, celebrating the feasting and merry-making; these are more akin to the ancient New Year carols, some of which still exist. In recent years more and more Christmas songs that have little to do with the Christmas story proper have sprung up, such as 'Rudolph the Red-Nosed Reindeer' and 'Jingle Bells', but there's nothing to beat the sensation of standing at a candlelit service and singing your heart out to one of the well-loved traditional melodies.

Carols themselves make good themes for Christmas decorations. Try creating paper or felt collages based on different ones, both traditional and modern, or create a centrepiece for your Christmas table – for instance, you could produce a dark green wreath decorated with gold music notes and white doves, with a gold and white angel in the centre, to illustrate the carol 'Hark! The Herald Angels Sing', or a paper cut-out version of 'The Twelve Days of Christmas'. Miniature musical instruments look very effective as tree decorations or hanging as mobiles; cut silhouettes out of card, then spray them gold or silver or cover them with glitter. Three-dimensional drums can easily be made out of old circular tins or boxes; fill them with sweets, baubles, Christmas cookies or small toys and use them as table centrepieces.

The theme for this mobile is the carol 'I Saw Three Ships'; use the diagram below to cut out the ship shapes. The mobile can be made with painted shapes, or with paper stained glass; if you are using paper stained glass, cut two black outline shapes for each ship so that you can sandwich the coloured tissue paper between them.

Traditional musical instruments such as these seem appropriate at Christmas time, perhaps because they remind us how ancient the tradition of carol-singing and seasonal merrymaking actually is.

In Victorian times, many Christmas trees were decorated with miniature musical instruments made from tin; you could continue this charming tradition by making your own instruments, forming them out of oven-hardening modelling material, or cutting two-dimensional versions out of card or foil and decorating them with felt pens, glitter, and gold and silver sequins.

The attractive shapes of these instruments would look effective reproduced large on a paper or fabric banner, for use at home or at a seasonal celebration in a church or school. Cut letters for a Christmas greeting out of felt or coloured foil and stick them onto the banner or paint them with a broad brush, then arrange the instruments around the edge. Alternatively, the trumpets and treble clefs would make a simple stencilled border. The herald's trumpet gives you the opportunity to add your own greeting on a Christmas card or banner.

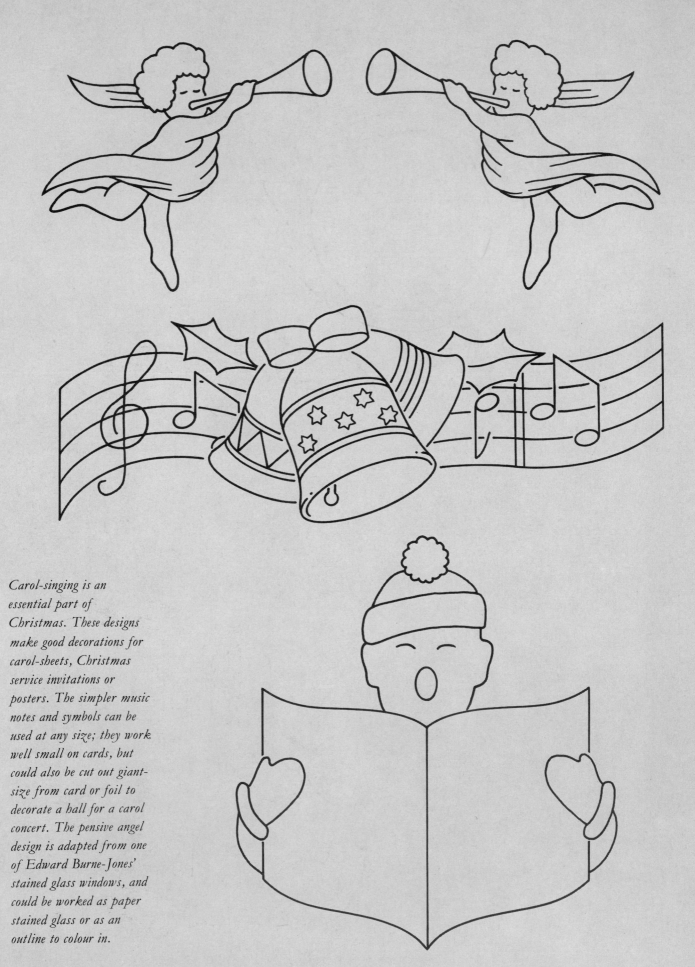

Carol-singing is an essential part of Christmas. These designs make good decorations for carol-sheets, Christmas service invitations or posters. The simpler music notes and symbols can be used at any size; they work well small on cards, but could also be cut out giant-size from card or foil to decorate a hall for a carol concert. The pensive angel design is adapted from one of Edward Burne-Jones' stained glass windows, and could be worked as paper stained glass or as an outline to colour in.

MATERIALS
AND
TECHNIQUES

PAPERCRAFT

Many different kinds of Christmas crafts can be produced in paper and card, and there are wonderful examples available in specialist shops, particularly around Christmas time. You can buy handmade papers produced from all kinds of fibres, including banana and rhododendron, as well as more conventional ones in a full spectrum of colours and a wide range of textures. The paper that you choose will depend very much on the particular craft you are doing, but for general cut-out and collage work, fairly firm, thick papers will work best; they lie flat, and are reasonably dense so that they can be decorated and glued without distorting very much. Foil 'papers' may be metal-based or paper-based; metal-based ones crease very easily, which can be an advantage for some crafts and a disadvantage for others! Foil papers come in many colours, and are very good for covering card shapes; stick the foil to the card before you cut out and assemble the shape, as it is difficult to add it to a three-dimensional structure.

Card is also available in many different colours, textures and finishes. Foil card comes in bright or subtle colours as well as the traditional gold and silver, and gives a wonderful effect for cut-outs, frames and models. Mounting card is a thick card which needs to be cut with a heavy-duty craft knife as it is very dense. Most other cards look their best if they are cut with a scalpel or craft knife rather than with scissors, which can bend or distort fine points or outlines. For models or structures which require folds, a special folding card, which creases cleanly and crisply, is available in some art supply shops.

Glues for paper and card depend on the kind of material you are using. Light papers are easily stuck with children's glue, in either liquid or stick form. Slightly heavier papers may need PVA glue or clear glue, while very firm card may require a hot glue gun. One disadvantage of foil (both paper and card) is that its surface is very easily marked, especially by different glues; clear glues in particular remove its colour instantly. For best results, use a clean stick glue and try to keep it away from the right side of the foil.

When you are using paper or card, mark the designs on the wrong side if possible. This will ensure that no marks show when the item is assembled. Remember that asymmetrical designs will need to be reversed if you are working on the wrong side.

Paper sculpture

Paper sculpture has become an art in itself, but simple versions can be used very effectively for Christmas and other crafts. It is a way of producing a slightly three-dimensional effect from two-dimensional pieces of paper or card by folding them in different directions.

The principle is just the same as making a fan by folding a flat piece of paper alternately upwards and downwards. The traditional colour scheme for paper sculpture is all-white, perhaps to show off the different angles and shapes, but the same principle can be used for paper or card of any colour. This technique is a good way of making textured foliage and flowers for paper and card wreaths and other decorations; the lines can be straight or curved, but should be relatively simple.

1 Mark the shapes of your design onto the back of firm paper or thin card, then cut out with sharp scissors or, even better, a craft knife.

2 For upward folds, mark the lines on the backs of the shapes in light pencil.

3 For downward folds, mark the lines in the same way on the fronts of the shapes.

4 Using a fine but slightly blunt tool such as a sewing bodkin or a fine bradawl, score along the marked lines with a firm stroke. If the lines are straight, use the point held up against a ruler as a guide.

5 Fold the paper or card along the lines with your fingertips to produce a three-dimensional effect.

6 You can add extra dimension to the shapes by bending them slightly as they are stuck onto their background.

Papier mâché

Papier mâché is an ancient craft which is enjoying quite a revival. Many people associate it with their schooldays, but it can actually produce very sophisticated effects. One great advantage is that the resulting shape can be finished in many different media. Newsprint is the traditional raw material for papier mâché because it is so absorbent, but if you want a pale finish to your item, you may not want to use newspaper. One way to overcome the problem is to use newspaper for most of the layers, then to finish off with several layers of white paper to provide a good final surface.

Always tear the paper for papier mâché rather than cutting it; tearing leaves an uneven, ragged edge which helps the paper to absorb the paste, and allows the different layers to blend into each other evenly.

1 Choose the object you are going to use as a mould. This should be a simple shape with no overhangs, otherwise you won't be able to remove the paper layers when they have dried. You can either build up the papier mâché on the inside or the outside of a mould; so, for instance, if you are using a mixing bowl, you could build up the layers inside it, or invert it and build up the layers on the outside.

2 In a large mixing bowl, make up a batch of wallpaper paste.

3 Tear up your chosen paper. If you are making a large flat item such as a tray, the paper can be in quite large pieces or strips; if you are making a small, rounded or detailed item, you will need quite small pieces.

Pleated circles of colourful wrapping paper are placed one above the other to make this Christmas tree. Glue them around a length of dowel secured inside a small flowerpot which is sprayed gold.

4 Separate the pieces of paper with your fingers so that you don't have bits sticking together, then place a batch of pieces or a few strips into your bowl of paste. If your paper is quite strong, you may need to leave the pieces to soak for a while so that they are fully pliable; they will go dark and translucent when they are saturated with paste. If you are using a very fine or absorbent paper, such as newsprint, you will only need to dip the paper pieces in and they are ready to use.

5 Put a thin covering of paper pieces over your mould. Keeping the pieces flat, overlap them and try to make sure that they are only one or two layers thick. Leave them until they are completely dry.

6 Continue to build up layers in the same way, letting each layer dry thoroughly before you add the next. The more layers you add, the stronger and more durable your final item will be.

7 When your papier mâché is as thick as you want it, check that it has dried right through and then gently prise it away from the mould.

8 Trim the edges of your papier mâché with sharp scissors or a craft knife, then decorate it in any way you want.

Paper stained glass

This is a very effective imitation of the real thing, and is superb for Christmas decorations. For the full effect, secure your finished item flat against a window pane and keep the curtains drawn back, so that during the day the sun will illuminate it for you inside, and during the evening your indoor lights will illuminate it for passers-by. Use a thick paper or thin card for the frame so that it keeps its shape, and coloured tissue paper or transparent wrapping material for the 'glass' so that the light can shine through. For ideas on design, use some of the motifs in the book, or copy designs from stained glass windows.

1 Draw your design full-size, making sure that each area of colour is supported by a surrounding 'leading' or frame which will be in black card.

2 Reversing it, transfer it to the wrong side of your black card. Go over the outlines with a pale crayon so that you can see the marks.

3 Using a scalpel or craft knife, cut away from the insides of the shapes where the colours will go.

4 To fill in a coloured area, tear or cut a piece of tissue paper so that it is about 1.3cm ($\frac{1}{2}$in) bigger all round than the shape it needs to fill. Working on the back of the black card, put a layer of stick glue all round the outline of the shape; don't put the glue on the tissue paper, as it is too fine and will tear. Lay the tissue paper shape over the glued area and press it into place.

5 Fill in all the other coloured areas in the same way.

Découpage

Découpage is a specialized kind of papercraft based on the principle of oriental lacquering. In lacquerwork, many layers of clear lacquer are used to seal and decorate items, producing an attractive and very highly polished surface finish.

Découpage is a way of sealing paper cut-outs under many layers of varnish, so that instead of having a textured surface where the cut edges of the paper fall, you have a completely smooth one.

Découpage was, until fairly recently, still quite a tricky and very time-consuming process, because you had to use slow-drying polyurethane varnish and spend weeks, if not months, building up enough coats. Now, spray varnishes dry quickly and allow you to do many coats in a day, speeding up the whole process enormously. Also, when slow-drying varnish was used, the whole craft had to be done in a dust-free environment, ideally in a spray-booth,

These unusual Christmas tree baubles were made from painted cotton balls and then covered with découpage motifs. High-gloss varnish gives them a good shine.

but, again, the quick-drying varnishes do not attract the dust in the same way and so can be used in any well-ventilated room. All kinds of items can be decorated with découpage; it works on firm cardboard, wood, metal and glass equally effectively.

1 Cut out the paper motifs that you are going to use to decorate your item.
2 Using PVA glue, stick them onto your item in a pleasing arrangement. Allow them to dry thoroughly. (Some people like to give their motifs a coating of dilute PVA medium at this stage, to make them slightly waterproof.)
3 Then place your decorated item on a newspaper in a well-ventilated room and cover it with a fine layer of spray polyurethane varnish. This is available in two finishes, matt and gloss; the gloss will give you the shiniest effect. Don't be tempted to apply a thick coat of varnish in order to save time. This will produce a mottled surface, which will defeat the object!

4 When the first layer is completely dry, continue with other layers in the same way. When you have sprayed four or five layers, sand the surface gently with some fine sandpaper or glass-paper; this helps to even out the ridges caused by the edges of the paper motifs. Don't sand too hard, or you might go through to the paper and start remov-ing the design.
5 Continue building up layers of var-nish in this way, sanding every three or four coats, until you have a completely smooth surface on your item.
6 Give the final layer of varnish an extra shine by polishing it with a soft cloth and a very small amount of furniture polish.

STENCILLING

Stencils can be used with various differ-ent types of paint, from fabric paint through to metallic sprays, but the principle is more or less the same with each method. The important thing is to avoid paint getting under the stencil itself, as most of the designs rely on a sharp outline for their full effect. Try stencils for mass-producing cards, wrapping paper, labels and deco-rations, as well as for decorating clothes and table linen.

1 Draw up the design for your stencil, remembering that you can't have any solid areas 'floating' inside coloured areas in the finished design; each 'island' of shape has to be attached to the 'mainland' of the stencil.
2 Transfer the design to the medium you are going to use for your stencil. If you only want to use the stencil a few times, card or even paper will do, but if you want a more durable stencil, try template plastic or stencil plastic.
3 Cut the centres out of the marked shapes, using a sharp craft knife.
4 Attach the stencil to the area you want to decorate. This can be done with

masking tape, or by spraying a very fine layer of spray glue onto the back of the stencil so that it adheres to the surface.

5 Brush, spray or splatter your paint through the stencil, making sure that your paint doesn't creep under the edges of the stencil shapes. To minimize this risk, use paint that is as dry as possible. If you are using a brush, brush from the edges of each shape inwards to the centre so that the bristles don't wander under the edges.

6 Remove the stencil carefully, check that no paint has transferred to the underside of the stencil, then reposition it further along or on a new background.

MODELLING

There are, of course, many different kinds of modelling. This section covers modelling in soft materials such as air-drying clay, salt dough, fondant icing and oven-hardening modelling material. The technique for modelling in each of these different media is very similar; they can all be moulded and shaped by hand, and given a variety of textures by, for example, tooling, stamping, rolling in cloth, pricking with cocktail sticks or pushing through a sieve. The main difference is in hardening. Air-drying clay, as its name suggests, eventually dries out when it is exposed to the air, while both salt dough and oven-hardening modelling material are baked to harden them. Fondant icing never gets truly hard, but does become slightly firmer when left to dry.

Oven-hardening modelling material

This is a synthetic modelling material which is available in many different colours; it can be used to make both large and small objects, which are then hardened by baking them in a domestic oven for a while. This type of modelling medium is very useful; it is already coloured, so you simply choose (or mix – the colours blend very well) the colour that you want for each part of your model. Colours can be marbled together as well for intriguing effects. Also, it doesn't shrink significantly as it bakes and the colours stay true, although they might darken a bit.

Oven-hardening modelling material is very versatile, and can take fine detail, which makes it suitable for small objects such as beads and jewellery as well as for large items such as candlesticks, table decorations and tree decorations. You can press fake jewels into it, and you can also buy special paints to enrich the colours with extra glitter or sheen. When coated with the appropriate varnish, objects become water-resistant. It is also possible to buy a flesh-toned version of this material, which makes it a good medium for modelling crib figures, angels and Father Christmas.

1 Choose the colour that you want to begin with, or that you want for the main part of your model, and cut a piece of a suitable size from the main block. If you can't find quite the colour you want, mix your own; if the colour is too dark, mix in a little white.

2 Roll and squeeze the piece of modelling material in your hands and fingers to warm it; this makes it more pliable and slightly more sticky.

3 Shape it as you wish. You can model with it directly, or plait it, twist it, texture it or roll it out and cut shapes from it like pastry.

4 When you want to join two pieces, press them together firmly.

5 When your model is complete, put it on a baking tray and bake in your oven, following the manufacturer's guidelines for temperature and baking time.

6 When baking is complete, take the models out of the oven and allow them to cool before embellishing them.

Salt dough modelling

Salt dough is another versatile medium, and lends itself to some beautiful projects. It has the great advantage that it is very cheap, and you can use it for all kinds of Christmas designs. It can be built up into three-dimensional models, or rolled out and cut with pastry cutters or a knife. If you want pastel colours on your finished model, colour the salt dough with food colouring or dissolved powder paint while you are rolling it; the colours will fade considerably during baking, and can either be left pale for a subtle effect, or restored with a coating of spray varnish. If you want brighter colours, paint your model with poster or acrylic paints once it has been baked. Needless to say, this dough is not pleasant to eat; you may need to warn children about this if they are helping you, as it looks very like ordinary pastry.

1 First, make your salt dough. You can make any amount of dough; just keep the proportions the same throughout. Use three measures of plain flour (don't use self-raising, as your models will swell), one measure of kitchen salt, one measure of water, and a small amount of dried wallpaper paste – about a heaped teaspoonful in an average mixing bowl full of salt dough. The wallpaper paste gives an extra stickiness to the dough and makes it easier to join bits while you are modelling. Mix the dry ingredients together thoroughly, then slowly add the water while stirring constantly to prevent lumps from forming.

2 Once all the ingredients are well combined, knead the dough thoroughly. This helps to eliminate air bubbles, and makes the dough pliable and easy to use. If the mixture is a little bit too sticky, add a small amount of flour. If it is a little bit too dry, add a very small amount of water.

3 When your dough is thoroughly pliable, put it in a plastic bag to stop it from drying out. If you want to colour different parts, pull out a bit of dough and knead some food colouring or dissolved powder paint into it. Put each colour into a separate plastic bag until you are ready to begin modelling.

4 Make your model in the usual way. You will find that with salt dough you can produce fine details as well as larger objects. Try not to make your salt dough models too thick, as this can cause problems while baking. If you are making figures, for instance, hollow them out inside the bases so that you are left with a thinner layer of salt dough.

5 When you want to join one piece of salt dough to another, moisten one area very slightly with water; this should enable the layers to stick.

6 When your model is finished, put it onto a piece of kitchen foil and bake it. Baking times vary enormously; what you are really doing is drying your model out rather than cooking it, rather like the principle of making meringues. Begin with the oven on cool at about $100°C$ (Gas Mark $\frac{1}{4}$) for half an hour or so, ideally leaving the oven door slightly open to allow the water to

Salt dough is perfect for modelling whimsical figures like this Santa Claus with his sack. He is painted in bright colours and then varnished.

evaporate, until the surface of the model begins to feel firm. If you are working on thin shapes such as flat Christmas tree decorations, this stage will be reached fairly quickly. If your shape is thicker, such as a wreath of leaves, it might need to stay at this temperature for about an hour. Once the surface starts to firm up, gradually increase the oven temperature to very hot, about 250°C (Gas mark 9), and bake until the model is bone dry; once again, this will take longer for thick models than for thin ones, and experience will tell you roughly how long different kinds of item take.

7 Once the model is baked and cool, it can be painted or varnished as you wish; the varnish makes it more durable, especially if you want the model to last a long time. Make sure that you varnish the back of a wreath or wall decoration as well as the front, otherwise it will absorb moisture through the back and eventually go soft and begin to crumble.

Air-drying clay

The principles for using air-drying clay are generally the same as for the other media, but this kind of clay does shrink, and therefore occasionally distort, as it dries out. The colour also fades, from dark grey to light grey, but as models made in this clay are generally designed to be painted, this is not usually a problem. Once the model is completely dry, use poster or acrylic paints to decorate it, then varnish it with polyurethane varnish.

Fondant icing

The principles of modelling with fondant icing are much the same as for other methods of modelling, except that, of course, you must make sure that you only use edible ingredients if the final result is to be eaten! Fondant icing can be bought in several different

colours, but if you want to use lots of colours in your modelling, the cheapest way is to buy a large block of the white icing and colour bits yourself as necessary. Fondant icing is very malleable and can be textured quite well in different ways, although it has a tendency to be sticky. If it becomes too sticky, roll the ball of icing or coat your hands in a little icing sugar. If it starts to dry out and become a little flaky, add a very small amount of water – often just a few drops are enough to make it more pliable again.

For joining one piece to another, moisten one surface with just a smear of water; this will be enough to make the two surfaces stick. While still fully pliable, the icing shapes can be decorated with dragées, sweets and other sprinkles, or you can add non-edible accessories such as a pastry brush for a snowman's broomstick. If you want a darker colour on your models, you can paint the finished shapes with food colouring instead of adding it to the mixture as you shape it. The shapes will dry out a little as they are exposed to the air, which makes them easier to handle, but they will always be a little soft, so treat them gently.

These traditional pink and white sugar mice are easy shapes to form from fondant icing. Their long tails are pieces of string.

MAKING WREATHS

Wreaths can be made from many different kinds of materials, such as dried flowers and seed-heads, foil or paper leaves and shapes, baubles and ribbons, but many of the principles remain the same whatever you are using to decorate your wreath, and no matter how small or large it is. Wreath bases can be bought in numerous shapes and sizes, including circles, ovals and heart-shapes, or you can make your own out of twisted twigs or basket canes. If you intend part of your wreath to show (as in the cherubs wreath on page 122), then make sure that it is attractive; spraying it gold, silver or a bright colour can be very effective, or you could spray it white as a contrast to darker foliage or bright decorations. If you want to give your wreath a basic covering so that anything that shows through will complement the decorations, try a wrapping of ribbon or bias-cut fabric for a fruit or bauble wreath, or a covering of sphagnum moss or dark yew branches for a wreath decorated with flowers or seed-heads.

Many of the larger items used to decorate wreaths can be wired for extra strength, whether these are plaster figures, baubles, pine-cones, large leaves or branches. Use a strong but flexible florists' wire; put it through any loops or stems on your decorations, then twist the wire firmly into position on the wreath. Candles can also be wired into position in the same way.

Once the background is established, work from the larger shapes to the smaller. Add small baubles, flower heads, leaves and other objects, attaching them in whichever way suits the materials best. You might want to wire them all, or jam stems between the twists of your wreath base, or use a hot glue gun to stick some items into place. Try to think of a final touch to add that element of individuality to your wreath: a paper or ribbon bow, a touch of gold or silver spray, a few tiny baubles dotted here and there, or perhaps a scattering of sequins.

Wreaths add a festive note to a table-setting or mantelpiece. This one is an informal arrangement made up of holly and other evergreens, with fir cones and teazels, and has simple cream candles which do not detract from the display.

SAFETY NOTE
Always remember to observe sensible safety precautions when you are using candles, especially on wreaths where lots of the other materials might be inflammable. If you are going to light the candles, don't leave them burning unattended, and don't let children play with them. Make sure that you blow them out or replace them before they burn down too far, and make sure, too, that no other decorations are hanging over the area where the candles are burning.

EMBROIDERY

Christmas embroideries are traditional in many countries; special decorated table linen is used for the festive meal, and runners and mats add a seasonal note all round the house. Many of the motifs in the book are ideal to translate into embroidery. Free-style embroidery can be worked on all kinds of fabrics, while for cross stitch you will need evenweave fabric such as aida or evenweave linen. For needlepoint, canvas is available in a range of mesh sizes for different items.

Transferring a design

If you would like to embroider one of the motifs in the book, first trace it from the page, then transfer it to your fabric with dressmaker's carbon paper in a suitable colour. You can enlarge or reduce the motifs on a photocopier first if you need them in a different size.

Using a chart

Needlepoint and cross-stitch designs are worked by following a chart. Each symbol in a square on the chart equals a needlepoint or cross stitch. Remember that the size of the canvas mesh plays an important part in the size of the finished embroidery. A pattern worked on 10-mesh canvas, for example, will be much bigger than the same pattern worked on 18-mesh canvas.

Finishing off

If your embroidery needs pressing, place it face down on a thick towel covered with a clean white cloth. Gently press from the back.

As the motifs charted in the book are quite small, needlepoint pieces may not need stretching back to shape. If they are slightly out of square, steam press gently from the back, adjusting the shape as you do so.

Any simple Christmas motifs can be worked in cross stitch onto evenweave fabric and used for special greetings cards. Mount your embroidery into card blanks, which are available in different colours and with different apertures.

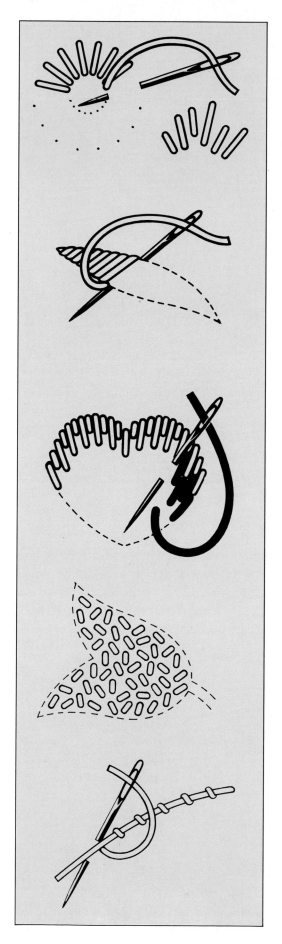

STITCH LIBRARY

FREE-STYLE STITCHES

STRAIGHT STITCH These are single stitches which can be worked in a regular fashion or just scattered at random. They can vary in length but should not be made too loose or long in case they snag.

SATIN STITCH This consists of straight stitches worked closely side by side across a shape. They can be upright or slanting, and may be padded slightly by working running stitch underneath. Satin stitch makes a beautiful smooth surface, and if shiny threads are used, reflects the light in an effective way.

LONG-AND-SHORT STITCH Beautiful shaded effects can be achieved with this stitch. It is very useful for filling shapes which are too big to be covered by satin stitch. Work the first row with alternate long and short stitches, following the outline of the shape. Fill in the following rows with stitches of similar lengths, keeping the embroidery smooth.

SEEDING This is a simple but useful filling stitch which gives a speckled effect. It is made up of short straight stitches scattered randomly over the fabric within a shape. For a varying density of tone, the stitches can be closely grouped in one area and spaced further apart in another.

COUCHING Lay a thread along the line of the motif. Then tie it down at regular intervals with another thread, using a contrasting colour or weight if required for effect.

SPLIT STITCH This is an outline stitch, but also works as a filling stitch where rows side by side make a fine flat surface. Bring the needle out at A, then take a small back stitch, piercing the thread with the needle tip as you pull it through.

STEM STITCH This is an ideal stitch for flower stems and outlines, but can also be arranged in rows side by side to fill in shapes. Working from left to right, make small even stitches along the outline, overlapping each stitch with the previous one as shown.

BACK STITCH A basic outline stitch, this can also be used in quilting instead of running stitch where a more defined line is required. Bring the needle through on the stitching line, take a small backward stitch and bring the needle out again a little further along. Take another backward stitch into the same hole as the previous stitch and so on.

FRENCH KNOTS Bring the thread through and, holding it down with your left thumb, twist the needle around it twice as shown in *fig. 1*. Keeping the thread taut, insert the needle back into the fabric where it first came out, as shown by the arrow. Pull the thread through and bring to the front again for the next French knot (*fig. 2*).

BULLION KNOTS Make a back stitch the length you wish the bullion knot to be, bringing just the needle point back through at the beginning of the stitch. Twist the thread around the needle so that it equals the length of the back stitch. Keeping the thread taut, pull the needle through and take it back to the beginning of the stitch (see arrow).

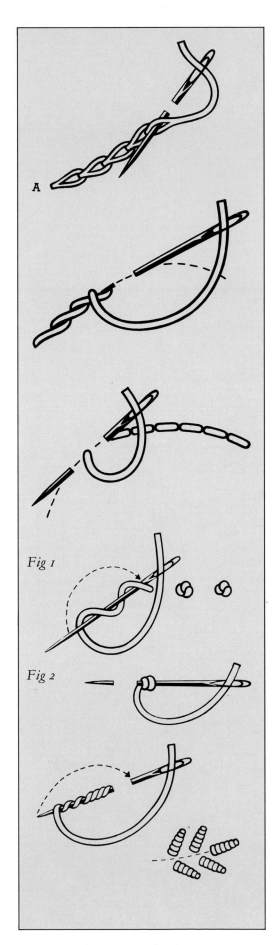

A

Fig 1

Fig 2

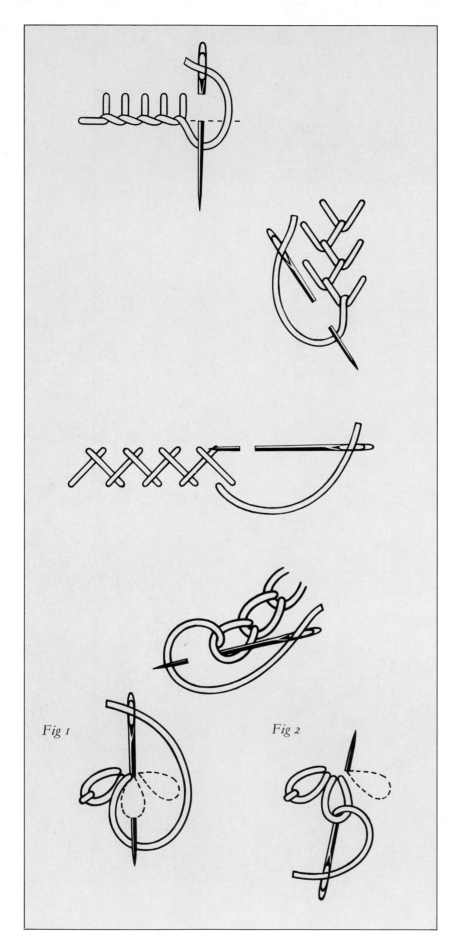

Fig 1

Fig 2

BLANKET STITCH Blanket stitch (or buttonhole stitch if closed up) is useful for working around appliqué shapes. Bring the thread through on the lower line, make a stitch from the upper to the lower line and, with the thread under the needle, pull the stitch through.

FEATHER STITCH Bring the thread through at the top centre. Insert the needle to the right and make a stitch downwards towards the centre, keeping the thread under the needle. Next, insert the needle to the left and make another stitch downwards and towards the centre with the thread under the needle.

HERRINGBONE STITCH Bring the thread through at the bottom. Moving slightly to the right, insert the needle from right to left along the top line and pull through, with thread below needle. Again moving to the right, make another stitch from right to left, with thread above needle.

CHAIN STITCH Chain stitch can be used as a filling stitch if worked in adjacent rows or as a spiral. It is also an outline stitch. Bring the thread through at the top of the line. Reinsert the needle in the same place and, holding down the loop with your thumb, bring the needle out a short way down. Pull the thread through to form a chain.

DETACHED CHAIN STITCH This is worked in the same way as chain stitch (*fig. 1*), but each loop is anchored down with a small stitch (*fig. 2*). The stitches can be worked singly, grouped into flower petals or scattered over the fabric like seeding.

COUNTED THREAD

CROSS STITCH The crosses are worked in two stages. First work a row of half cross stitch from right to left (*fig. 1*), then work back the other way to complete the crosses (*fig. 2*). The top arm of each cross stitch should slope in the same direction.

NEEDLEPOINT STITCHES

TENT STITCH Tent stitch can be worked either in diagonal rows as in *figs. 1 and 2* or in horizontal rows as in *figs. 3 and 4*. The former method is preferable, where possible, as it prevents the canvas from being distorted by the stitching.

HALF CROSS STITCH This needlepoint stitch resembles tent stitch but is worked differently. It is useful when embroidering with a thick yarn, as it is not as bulky. Each diagonal stitch is worked over one canvas intersection and the stitches on the back are vertical.

BRICK STITCH This consists of vertical stitches worked in staggered rows. In *fig. 1* long and short stitches are worked alternately. In *fig. 2*, the next and all subsequent rows interlock neatly with the one above.

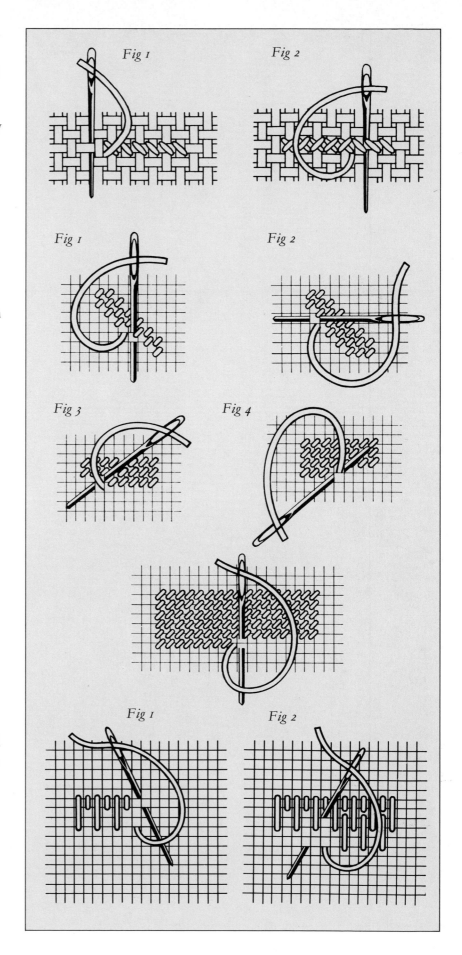

INDEX

ACKNOWLEDGMENTS

All craft items designed and made by Gail Lawther except the following: pages 11, 45, 81, 100, 102, designs by Valerie Janitch; pages 12, 34, 42, 52, 63 (top), 71, 90 (top), 91, 93, 112, 120, 121 (top), 123, designs by Kerrie Dudley; page 22, design by Gail Lawther on a cake made by Christopher Lawther; page 70, made by Gail Lawther after an idea by Angela Besley; page 113 (bottom) stitched by Gail Lawther after a design by Patrick Lawther.

The photographs on the following pages were taken by: Steve Tanner, pages 12, 42, 52, 63 (top), 71, 90 (top), 91, 93, 112, 120, 121 (top), 123, 130, 132, 134, 136; Di Lewis, pages 11, 45, 81, 100, 102, 137; Patrick McLeavey page 135.

With grateful thanks to Philip and Tacey Ltd, North Way, Andover, Hants SP10 5BA, who provided many of the craft items used in this book.

The publisher would like to thank the following for the loan of props for photography:

Paperchase
213 Tottenham Court Road
London W1P 9AF
For mail order or information on location of branches, tel: 071 580 8496

Nice Irma's Ltd
46 Goodge Street
London W1P 1FJ
Tel: 071 580 6921
For mail order tel:
081 343 7610